THE
ANALYTICAL
ENGINE

D0760706

THE ANALYTICAL ENGINE

Computers—
Past, Present and Future

Newly Revised

JEREMY BERNSTEIN

WILLIAM MORROW AND COMPANY, INC.
New York 1981

Library of Congress Cataloging in Publication Data

Bernstein, Jeremy, 1929-
    The analytical engine.

    "Morrow quill paperbacks."

    Bibliography: p.
    Includes index.

    1. Computers.   2. Electronic digital computers.
I. Title.
QA76.B45   1981b   001.64   80-29428
ISBN 0-688-00484-9
ISBN 0-688-00488-1 (pbk.)

Printed in the United States of America

First Morrow Quill Paperback Edition

1 2 3 4 5 6 7 8 9 10

BOOK DESIGN BY MICHAEL MAUCERI

The author wishes to thank the following authors and publishers for permission to quote from the following copyrighted material.

"The Philosophy of Niels Bohr" by Aage Petersen, in the September 1963 issue of the *Bulletin of the Atomic Scientists.* © Copyright 1963 by Educational Foundation for Nuclear Science, Inc.

To my parents

Preface

Niels Bohr had a wonderful way of expressing and criticizing ideas through his humor—"just some little jokes." Recently, I came across one of the stories Bohr loved in an article on his philosophy written by Aage Petersen, who was his assistant in the last years of Bohr's life. As Petersen tells it, "In an isolated village there was a small Jewish community. A famous rabbi once came to the neighboring city to speak and, as the people of the village were eager to learn what the great teacher would say, they sent a young man to listen. When he returned he said, 'The rabbi spoke three times. The first talk was brilliant; clear and simple. I understood every word. The second was even better; deep and subtle. I didn't understand much but the rabbi understood all of it. The third was by far the finest; a great and unforgettable experience. I understood nothing and the rabbi himself didn't understand much either.'"

About the subject of computers, I feel somewhat the way the young man felt about the rabbi. There is a part that I have come to understand on my own (the interested reader will find a bibliography, listing those references that were especially useful to me in this process); there is a part that computer experts have explained to me; and, finally, there is a part that involves things on the frontier of research and not yet completely understood. I have tried to warn the reader when things become speculative—and often these were for me among the most fascinating things to learn and write about —by sprinkling the appropriate sections liberally with "probably's" and "perhaps's."

This book and the articles in *The New Yorker* that it is based on were written with the help of many people. In the first place, most of the people still active in the field who are mentioned in the book have read parts of the manuscript, and I am immensely grateful to them for the time they took in explaining their work and for seeing to it that my version of it was as free of error as possible. In addition to this large group of computer experts, I would like to thank Thomas J. Deegan of I.B.M., who became fascinated by the problem of trying to do a serious article on computers for a wide audience of laymen and who helped me, for nearly a year, to gather a wide range of material. I am also grateful to Robert Gerdy of *The New Yorker* editorial staff for his constant and patient guidance, criticism, and help in what appeared to me at the start to be an almost impossible job in shaping and clarifying the very difficult material in the articles. Finally, I am grateful to William Shawn, the editor of *The New Yorker*, for encouraging me to try to write about such a complex scientific subject for a magazine whose readership is composed of people who are predominantly nonscientists.

Preface to the Second Edition

Most writers—and I am no exception—have a considerable affection for their literary offspring. This book—*The Analytical Engine*—has a special place for me, since it is the first book I ever wrote. Indeed, at the time I wrote it—now almost twenty years ago —as a series of articles for *The New Yorker*, it did not occur to me that it was a book. This was suggested to me by my then editor, the late Robert Gerdy, who, in fact, actually found a publisher for it and helped me take the first steps into what was then for me an entirely new domain. His contributions to the original articles were immense, something that I was pleased to acknowledge in the preface to the original edition, and which I am equally pleased to acknowledge, once again, in his memory.

I worked on the articles with Gerdy for nearly a year from 1962 to 1963. At this time, computers were in their infancy and a great many people were afraid of them. Hence what I tried to do was to demystify the machines. As far as I know, the original articles were the first to appear in a national magazine in which a serious attempt was made to explain things from first principles in such a way that a nonscientific reader could come to grips with these then new and remarkable machines. What I tried to do at that time was to show that, basically, these machines were *merely* amplifications of human arithmetic skills. They are surely that but, as we now know, they are much more. Computers manipulate symbols of which numbers are only a special case. They can be programmed to play chess, to prove geometrical theorems, to create new programs, and even to reason by analogy. And the end is nowhere in sight.

Moreover, powerful computers are now becoming common household appliances; something that no one visualized as a possibility twenty years ago. Adolescents now know more about programming than most scientists knew when I wrote my articles. In this edition of my book, I have tried to explain how this has come about. I have also tried to give some flavor of what is now known as "artificial intelligence"—the outer fringes of computer science. What I have *not* done is enlarge the format of the original book. It was originally intended to be a concise overview of the history and development of computing machines—"analytical engines" in Charles Babbage's luminous phrase—and this is what it shall remain.

In preparing this edition I would like to acknowledge the help of Douglas Hofstadter, Gloria Poetto, Bernie Rosen, and, above all, of my friend and mentor in these matters, Marvin Minsky.

THE
ANALYTICAL
ENGINE

1.

My first contact with large electronic computing machines occurred in the winter of 1962 when I took a course in FORTRAN programming at New York University. This was, however, by no means my first contact with machine-assisted numerical computation. In fact, my Ph.D. thesis in theoretical physics at Harvard in 1955 involved, among other things, the computation of about seventy-five numerical integrals. An "integration" simply means finding the area under a given curve. For the so-called "elementary functions" this procedure can be carried out painlessly by simply looking up in a table the relevant formula for the integral and then plugging in any numbers that might be relevant to the problem at hand. In my case the functions were not elementary but existed only in tabular form as numerical values in a table. These tables themselves had a curious history since many of them dated from the Depression days of the 1930's during which otherwise unemployed mathematicians were given jobs by the Works Progress Administration—the old Roosevelt WPA—to hand-tabulate these functions. Both the WPA mathematicians and I made use of electrically operated hand calculators with wheels and gears which were turned by motors. These machines had no "memories"—there was no way of storing data except by writing it on sheets of paper as the computation proceeded, something that rapidly became, at least in my case, a terrible mess. Each numerical integral took me several days to do and it was almost impossible, working alone as I was, to be sure that there were no mistakes. It was a very tedious business and, worse than that, a tremendous waste of time. Even then, if I had had access to the first generation of vacuum tube computers, one of which was available at nearby M.I.T., I could have reduced this job to a matter of days instead of months. Nowadays I would be able to carry the whole thing out in short order on one of the more elaborate pocket calculators which sell for about a hundred dollars.

During the next few years after my Ph.D. I worked as the "house theorist" for the Harvard Cyclotron Laboratory and did many more numerical calculations still using hand computers. But, by this time, the use of electronic computers for scientific work was becoming much more widespread, although very few scientists knew how to program the machines. This dark art was the province of a specially trained group of people—the programmers—often skilled mathematicians. Very few of the physicists I knew knew much about it. It was only in 1962, when my friend Gerald Feinberg, now chairman of the Physics Department at Columbia, took a programming course and told me how simple it was that I decided to try it for myself. As everyone now knows the first thing one learns in dealing with such a machine is getting over the language barrier. The early machines had to be programmed in their own "machine language" and this was so remote from, say English, that it required an expert to manufacture even the simplest programs. What Feinberg and several other colleagues persuaded me of is that there had been a great revolution in programming— that the job had been made much easier by the invention of several new languages, which stuck remarkably close to the words and symbols of conventional mathematical language, and which the machines more or less translated for themselves. In fact, I was assured that even if one had only a vague idea of how a modern computer worked, one could learn to communicate with it—to some degree, at least—without an interpreter. I was also told that the appropriate language for the sort of scientific computation I customarily ran up against was called FORTRAN (for "Formula Translation") and that a good many universities occasionally offered short, intensive courses in it, rather like cram courses in Italian or French. New York University, where I then taught, had a computing center, which was part of the Courant Institute of Mathematical Sciences. It offered short FORTRAN courses three times a year, and I decided to enroll in one of them. As it turned out, I found that learning something about FORTRAN was an excellent introduction to the subject of computers in general.

Before going to the first lecture, I had assumed that all my fellow FORTRAN students would be professional scientists or engineers, but, in a quick survey, our instructor, an operations associate at the Courant Institute named Howard L. Walowitz, discovered that the class included a librarian and also several women from the university's Department of Nurse Education, who were writing theses involving detailed analyses of medical statistics. Although a few of the students had taken FORTRAN courses elsewhere and were just brushing up, most of us had no knowledge whatsoever of the language. However, FORTRAN programming is simple enough to learn so that within a couple of days most of us had learned enough about its elements to set up a simple problem and get an answer back from the machine.

The first step in programming is, needless to say, to write down something on something, and Mr. Walowitz started out by showing us the kind of sheet we would write on—a blank FORTRAN coding form. This is a piece of pale-green paper, the size of typewriter paper and ruled off into about fifteen hundred rectangles, each of which can be filled in with a digit, a letter, or a punctuation mark. We were then given a coding form with an easy "model" problem, one that obviously didn't require a multi-million-dollar computer—a simple income-tax computation, in which the tax was to be computed according to the formula:

$$\text{TAX} = 22\% \quad (\text{GROSS INCOME} - \$600.00 \times$$
$$\text{NUMBER OF EXEMPTIONS})$$

At first glance, a FORTRAN program appears somewhat forbidding, but once one understands the role that the different phrases play, one begins to appreciate how precise and even elegant they are. Slightly abbreviated, our model FORTRAN program for doing the tax went like this:

1 READ INPUT TAPE 5,
GROSS, EXMP
TAX = 0.22 • (GROSS — EXMP • 600.0)
IF (TAX) 2,3,3
2 TAX = 0.0
3 WRITE OUTPUT TAPE 6,
GROSS, EXMP, TAX
GO TO 1

It was easy to get the impression from seeing a command like the first one that the machine would respond to any English command—READ PROUST, say. Actually, FORTRAN consists of only a limited number of phrases, which can be put together to convey the sequence of steps needed in solving a great variety of mathematical problems. Most large computers at that time stored data on reels of magnetic tape, and in this instance the READ command informed the machine that it would find the appropriate data—a set of figures for gross income and exemptions—on Magnetic Tape 5.

Second came the formula, written very much the way one would normally write it, the main exception being that a few of the symbols were changed to avoid ambiguity. Thus:

$$\text{TAX} = 0.22 \cdot (\text{GROSS} - \text{EXMP} \cdot 600.0)$$

What appeared next was one of the most powerful FORTRAN statements—one that illustrates the "decision-making" ability of a modern computer:

$$\text{IF } (\text{TAX}) \; 2,3,3$$

This statement tells the machine how to proceed after computing the tax, depending on whether the answer is a negative number, zero, or a positive number. If the answer is negative, the machine is to go Instruction 2, or:

$$\text{TAX} = 0.0$$

There is no such thing as a negative tax, and Instruction 2 says that if EXMP · 600 should exceed GROSS, the machine is to write out the tax as zero. In this case, practically speaking, one negative answer would mean the same as another—no tax—so the prcgrammer has no interest in just what the negative number is.

If the tax came out either zero or positive, the machine was to proceed to Instruction 3, which told it to write out the actual result of the tax computation on another tape. This tape was used to run a high-speed automatic printer, which then printed out the whole computation on paper.

GO TO 1 instructs the machine to go back to the beginning of the program—that is, to start over again with the next set of figures on Tape 5.

This sequence of instructions enabled the machine to compute the tax once the programmer had supplied sets of numerical values for the variables GROSS and EXMP. These values were written under the heading DATA, just below the instruction sequence. In due course they were transcribed onto Magnetic Tape 5. The program and the data are separate entities, and once the programmer has set up a program, he can use it any time he provides the data.

At the next lecture, we received our first homework assignment, and from it I learned that although FORTRAN looks simple, it is full of nuances. Our problem had to do with mortgage amortization and, like the tax computation, it came down to evaluating a formula—that is, finding the numerical values corresponding to the abstract variables—but this formula was somewhat more complex than the tax formula. We were advised to prepare a "flow chart" before we actually began to write out the program. A flow chart is a diagram illustrating the logical "flow" of steps that must be taken to solve a problem. In preparing it one has to think out, in proper order, the various mathematical and logical operations that one would perform in solving the problem on one's own. On one's own, of course, one often takes operations for granted and performs them almost without thinking. A machine cannot be expected to take anything for granted, and though the process of diagramming the steps is somewhat tedious, one learns after making a few attempts at writing a program without preparing a flow chart, that it is an invaluable way to keep the outline of the program straight. However, the program itself must be made up out of the set phrases and grammatical constructions that constitute the FORTRAN language. So, hav-

ing decided on the appropriate sequence of operations, and having outlined these on the flow chart,
one must find the FORTRAN expressions that will convey one's commands to the machine. Finding just
the right expressions to do the job is a little like
putting together a jigsaw puzzle, and once one gets
the hang of it, it can be a good deal of fun. But
FORTRAN has a very finicky grammar; if one leaves
out a comma where the rules say there must be a
comma, the machine will simply not accept the
program. It was only after three or four unsuccessful
attempts that I was able to write out a program with
all of the grammatical details correct, and when I
got back the printed results of my first computation
—the printout—I had a feeling of satisfaction of having communicated with the machine that reminded
me of the way I felt when, after a week of French
lessons in Paris, I discovered that I was able to en-
gage in useful, if limited, conversations with my
concierge.

In doing our second homework problem, which
was a lot harder than the first, I learned what happens when a faulty FORTRAN program gets put onto
the machine. I had prepared what seemed to me an
absolutely foolproof green sheet and had given it to
the keypunch operators. After a while, I got my printout, which began with the date and with the title
"709/7090 FORTRAN DIAGNOSTIC PROGRAM RESULTS."
Next came one of the formulas I had written out,
followed by the terse comment TOO MANY LEFT
PARENTHESES. (FORTRAN grammar, like any other, de-
mands that left and right parentheses balance.) I
looked at the formula and saw that the keypunch
operator had taken a slash symbol, which indicates

division, for a left parenthesis. To the machine, the formula appeared as:

$$\text{STDV} = (\text{SUM (GN)} \cdot\cdot .5$$

It should have been:

$$\text{STDV} = (\text{SUM} / \text{GN}) \cdot\cdot .5$$

When I asked what had happened, I was told something about the steps the machine takes after it receives a FORTRAN program. It first scans the program for any simple grammatical error, like leaving out a comma. If everything seems in order, it normally proceeds to translate the FORTRAN into machine language—a process known as compiling—and then to carry out the commands, just as a person given an instruction in a foreign language would translate it before acting on it. If the machine does pick up some errors in the first scan, it does not go on with the translation but prints out a sheet with diagnostic messages that call attention to the mistakes. Near the bottom of my printout, I found a set of messages that almost seemed to grumble:

ILLEGAL USE OF PUNCTUATION . . . SOURCE
PROGRAM ERROR . . . NO COMPILATION . . .
EXECUTION DELETED.

When I pointed these out to Mr. Walowitz, he said he often wished that the machine would simply correct the mistake, go on with its business, and leave one alone. At the end of the sheet, there was a notation that it had taken the machine some thirty-six seconds to locate the mistake. By present-day standards this is extremely slow. The machine that we were working on—an I.B.M. 7090—which was a very advanced machine for its day, was capable of something like one hundred thousand operations per second. At the present time, the fastest machine now operating is the Control Data Corporation's CYBER 205, which can carry out eight hundred million arithmetical operations per second. Any modern computer would now take only a fraction of a second to locate a mistake like this. Most of the homework problems that we did—they were relatively simple machine computations, to be sure—took less than a minute of machine time. During this time, the machine made the translation from the FORTRAN program into machine language; executed the machine-language program, using whatever data one had supplied; and put the result of the computation onto magnetic tape. None of the problems we did would take more than a fraction of a second to run on a modern machine.

Correcting the program, in my case of ILLEGAL USE OF PUNCTUATION, amounted simply to having the keypunch operator prepare a new card—something that was extremely easy to do, since only one symbol had to be changed. The operator set the keypunch to reproduce the original card up to the errant parenthesis, then keyed in the slash symbol by hand, and finally set the keypunch to reproduce the rest of the original card. These punch cards have now been replaced by magnetic tapes or disks of which more later. One can make corrections like this simply by retyping the program on the tape or disk. The simple programs of the type we were running can be displayed on a television screen and be easily corrected as one goes along.

Most of the errors that the FORTRAN diagnostic program picks up have to do with punctuation. Of course, it is quite possible (even customary) to make other kinds of mistakes—in logic, for example —and the machine will usually not pick these up, though it may catch mistakes that fall somewhere between punctuation and logic. For example, I once wrote a program in which I labeled a statement 9070 and later referred to it as 9060. The machine reacted by printing out:

THE FOLLOWING FORMAT STATEMENTS, THOUGH REFERRED TO, HAVE BEEN OMITTED FROM THE SOURCE PROGRAM . . . 9060

When I asked why the machine didn't diagnose a wider variety of errors, I was told that it would just be a waste of the machine's time. It is much more economical to have the machine spot errors in punctuation and to use the human programmer to spot the more subtle ones.

During the next two weeks, our homework became more and more difficult. One of our most interesting tasks was to program the machine to arrange several hundred numbers in descending order—a problem that involved several uses of the FORTRAN IF statement, which we had been introduced to our first day in class. This time, we used IF statements to instruct the machine to arrange and rearrange the numbers after subtracting them from one another and seeing whether the result was positive, negative, or zero. The exercise also gave us a detailed introduction to FORTRAN DO statements, sometimes known as DO loops. Often in the course of a computation one wishes to repeat a process several times in sequence.

A simple, if not very striking, example would be multiplying all of the numbers from 1 to 10, one after the other, by the number 3. One could, of course, write a FORTRAN program involving ten separate multiplication instructions, but this would be a nuisance—and more than a nuisance—if, instead of ten multiplications, one wanted, say, ten thousand. The whole set of instructions can be compressed into two simple commands:

$$\text{DO } 5, \text{ I} = 1, 10$$
$$5 \text{ M (I)} = 3 \cdot \text{I}$$

The DO statement here tells the machine to do Instruction 5 for the ten values, and Instruction 5 tells it to multiply the integer I, whatever it happens to be, by 3.

Our class also learned how to make use of "subroutines." In arithmetic work, certain special operations—like taking a square root or a logarithm—are likely to be used many times, and although it would be quite possible to write out in FORTRAN the detailed steps for, say, taking a square root, it is much more economical to write out, once and for all, a square-root program, store it on magnetic tape, and bring it into a calculation whenever it is needed. Computing the square root of quantity F can be called for simply by writing:

$$\text{SQRT (F)}$$

Every computer manufacturer now supplies its own library of subroutines. Even the modern programmable pocket calculators have subroutine libraries that are more elaborate than what was available when I took my course.

Although I hardly qualified as an expert programmer at the end of the two-week course, I did have some understanding of what sort of problems FORTRAN can help one solve, and while none of our homework assignments sprang directly from physics, they involved similar types of calculations, and I felt some confidence in my ability to set up my own problems for the computer. All the time I was taking the course, however, I had an uneasy feeling; what the machine could do became impressively clear to me, but I kept wondering how it did it. When I finished the course, I decided to find out something about the machines, their history, and what we can expect of them in the future.

2.

Nowadays, the ability to perform arithmetical computations is shared by most educated people. In doing computations, memory certainly plays an important role. If one did not know the multiplication table by heart, the simplest arithmetic would become a nightmare, and we take it for granted that just about everybody does know it. This widespread knowledge, however, is quite a recent phenomenon. In a brilliant essay entitled "A Brief History of Computation," written in 1953 and published in a book called *Faster Than Thought*, Dr. B. V. Bowden, of Ferranti, Ltd., a British computer-manufacturing firm, notes:

A few hundred years ago the art of computation was neither commonly understood nor widely practised. In 1662, Pepys, who was then in charge of the contracts branch of the Admiralty, found it necessary to put himself to school, and to rise by candlelight at four o'clock in the morning in order to learn his multiplication tables. He had been to Cambridge, and was, by the standards of his time, a well-educated man, [and] in later life he became President of the Royal Society and a friend of Newton, but when he was Clerk of the Acts he found himself quite unable to understand the simple computations which had to be done when buying timber for the King. In those days school boys seldom went beyond "two times two."

Apparently, his efforts were not in vain, for, as Dr. Bowden notes, in December, 1663, Pepys wrote in his diary: "My wife rose anon, and she and I all the afternoon at arithmetique, and she able to do additions, subtractions and multiplications very well, and so I purpose not to trouble her yet with divisions, but show her the use of Globes."

The ability to calculate rapidly varies a great deal, and has nothing at all to do with the ability to grasp the abstractions of higher mathematics; mathematicians, by and large, are not outstanding computers, nor is computational skill vital for creative work in mathematics. In the summer of 1961, I had an opportunity to work with Mr. William Klein, who was then programmer and numerical analyst for CERN (Centre Européen pour la Recherche Nucléaire) in Geneva, and who must be one of the fastest human computers who has ever lived. I was spending the summer doing physics at CERN and had been working with a friend on a problem. After a week or so, we produced an algebraic formula that seemed admirable to us in many respects, and we wanted to evaluate it. CERN had at that time a large Ferranti Mercury computer, and since neither of us then knew anything about programming, we asked for help. Enter Mr. Klein. Mr. Klein was, and is, a short, kindly, youthful-looking man. He was born in Amsterdam in 1912. He looked at our formula for a few seconds, muttering to himself in Dutch, and then gave us numerical estimates for several of the more complex parts of it. Doing this, he said, helped set up the program for the computer in the most efficient way. I had heard about Mr. Klein's almost incredible ability, and I asked him whether he had considered evaluating our whole expression in his head. He told me that it would involve much too much work and that he was quite glad to turn the job over to the machine. Watching Mr. Klein at work made a deep impression on me, and I was delighted to find something about him in another of Dr. Bowden's essays, this one called "Thought and Machine Processes." Dr. Bowden writes:

[Mr. Klein] knows by heart the multiplication tables up to 100×100, all squares up to 1000×1000, and an enormous number of odd facts, such as $3937 \times 127 = 499999$, which are very useful to him, and seem to arise instantly in his mind when they are needed. In addition, Mr. Klein [who knows the logarithms of numbers up to 150 to fourteen decimal places] can work out sums like compound interest by "looking up" the logs in his head, after factorizing the numbers he is using, if need be. He has also learned enough about the calendar to be able to give the day of the week corresponding to any specified date in history.

Dr. Bowden goes on:

Mr. Klein multiplies numbers of up to six digits faster in his head than an ordinary man can do by using a desk calculating machine. For example, he wrote down the products of six pairs of 3-digit numbers in nine seconds; an experienced calculating machine operator took a minute to do the same calculations.

Mr. Klein multiplied

$$1\ 388\ 978\ 361 \times 5\ 645\ 418\ 496$$
$$= 7\ 841\ 364\ 129\ 733\ 165\ 056$$

completely in his head, a calculation which involved twenty-five multiplications each of two 2-digit numbers and twenty-four additions of 4-digit numbers—forty-nine operations in all—in sixty-four seconds. . . . A dozen of us tried it [and] the times we took varied between six and sixteen minutes, and all our answers were wrong excepting one.

When I asked Mr. Klein about this feat in 1961, he told me, jokingly, that since he had come to rely on computers, he was slightly out of practice, and Dr. Bowden's multiplication would take him a full two minutes. At any rate, phenomenal ability in

computation apparently runs in the Klein family,
for Dr. Bowden adds:

> Mr. William Klein's brother Leo, who died at
> the hands of the Gestapo during the war, was
> almost as good a computer as William and a
> better mathematician. Dr. Stokvis of Amsterdam
> made a psychological study of the brothers; he
> found that although their performances were
> very similar their methods of operation were
> quite different. For example, Mr. William Klein
> remembers numbers "audibly"; he mutters to
> himself as he computes, he can be interrupted
> by loud noises, and if he ever does make a mistake
> it is by confusing two numbers which sound alike.
> Leo, on the other hand, remembered things
> "visually"; and if he made a mistake it was by
> confusing digits which look alike.

A few years ago Mr. Klein retired from CERN and
is now living in Amsterdam. However, we have
kept in touch and, over the years, I have learned
a good deal about his life. His father was a physician with no special arithmetical abilities, but
by the age of six Klein had already fallen in love
with numbers. When he was nine he came upon the
notion of factoring numbers. He learned the multiplication process sort of backwards: he did not learn
the tables but began by taking large numbers and
dividing them into smaller ones. He recalls that he
got into trouble in elementary school when he tried
to convince his teacher that this was really a better
way to learn multiplication. When he was twelve,
he entered the Vossiusgymnasium in Amsterdam and

there had the good fortune to run into a teacher who became interested in his extraordinary abilities. This teacher gave him a book whose title in English translation would be *Secrets of Lightning Calculators*. From it Klein learned that there was something called a logarithm which enabled one to compute roots. He begged his teacher to show him logarithms. At first, the teacher said that Klein was too young but finally he relented and one Friday gave him a logarithm table. On the following Monday, the teacher asked him how he had made out and discovered to his astonishment that, over the weekend, Klein had memorized the logarithms of the first 150 numbers to five decimal places. This was not exactly what the teacher had in mind.

What Klein's father had in mind, meanwhile, was for his son to abandon his numbers and become a physician. What Klein had in mind was to become some kind of a circus performer, displaying his ability with numbers. As one might imagine, he ended up in medical school, which he hated. In 1937, his father died and Klein and his brother inherited a sizable sum of money. Klein dropped out of medical school immediately and lived a carefree life in Amsterdam until the Nazis came. He barely escaped from the SS and was hidden for a period by a fireman and his family. After the war, Klein, with his money gone, began to perform working on his own. At first he called himself Fakir Ali ben Achmed, but soon became convinced that this was somewhat silly. He abandoned the turban and beard of the Fakir and changed his working name to Pascal in honor of the French savant who invented the first truly mechanical calculator. For the next five years he performed

in the Netherlands, Belgium, and France. In Paris
he used to perform on the street near a metro station.
He once remarked to me that the two natural
enemies of street performers are the rain and the
police and that it was the latter that, in 1951, finally
put an end to his career in France. For a while
Mr. Klein was employed as a computer in Amsterdam's Stichting Mathematische Centrum but he
found this so boring that after two years of it he went
back to performing. Among other things he was fea-
tured on an English music hall program along with
an armless man and a daredevil bicycle act. Klein
was billed as "The Man with the £10,000 Brain."
"It was a smashing time," he told me.

In 1958, Klein came to the attention of the late
C. J. Bakker, a Dutch physicist who was then director
general of CERN. Klein asked Bakker whether there
was any possibility of his getting a job at CERN as a
numerical analyst and recalled that Bakker replied,
"I don't know exactly. I am just the director general."
In any event Klein was hired on a provisional basis
for three months, but after four weeks had proved
so useful that he was offered a permanent job. As I
have indicated, this was at a time when very few
physicists knew much of anything about computer
programming. To be of service to them Klein learned
programming, but he had, as I mentioned, the un-
usual capacity of being able to do bits and pieces
of a program in his head. He also knew by heart, or
could figure out instantly, the numerical values of
sines, cosines, logarithms and the like. I recall that
one summer when I had an office next to his at CERN
I used to pop in and ask him for various values of

these functions when they came up in my work. Now, of course, one can find these values by pressing a button on a pocket calculator. Indeed, over the years, physicists almost universally have learned to program computers and so there was less and less room for Klein's talents. So, for the five or six years before he retired in 1976 his main involvement with CERN was in its public-relations program. For example, he gave a summer lecture for students which was one of the annual events at the laboratory.

Klein's abilities have, if anything, improved over the years. He set a speed record—duly noted in the *Guinness Book of World Records*—on August 27, 1976, for mentally calculating the perfect seventy-third root of a five hundred-digit number. It took him two minutes and forty-three seconds. But in April of 1979 he got this down to two minutes and nine seconds. He also improved his record for calculating the perfect thirteenth root of a hundred-digit number, which used to be three minutes and thirty-seven seconds. (Oddly, this computation is harder than computing the seventy-third root of a five hundred-digit number, the reason being that the answer to the thirteenth-root problem contains eight digits, while the answer to the seventy-third root problem contains only seven—a difference that makes the mental arithmetic simpler.) In a demonstration at Brown University in the fall of 1979 he did the same sort of calculation in three minutes and twenty-five seconds. He had done a similar calculation the previous night, but some of the Brown professors expressed disbelief—a common phenomenon when one sees Klein at work—and they maintained that Klein had probably memorized the answer in advance. Klein then invited them to provide their own number on which he set his new record.

Unlike, for example, the great early nineteenth century mathematician Karl Friedrich Gauss, who was both a calculating prodigy and one of the most creative mathematicians who ever lived, Klein has never been much interested in most branches of pure mathematics. He has studied some number theory, but what he really enjoys doing is arithmetic computation. Given his abilities it is easy to see why, though most of us have feelings about arithmetical calculation closer to those expressed by the German polymath Gottfried Wilhelm Leibniz when he wrote in 1671, "It is unworthy of excellent men to lose hours like slaves in the labor of calculation which could safely be relegated to anyone else if machines were used."

Calculating machines have been of two fundamental types—analog and digital. The analog machines represent numbers by some analogous quantity, such as length or size. A child might learn to add by assembling blocks of various sizes; a block of a given size would be the analog of 1, a block twice the size the analog of 2, and so on. The most widely known analog calculator is the ordinary slide rule, which was invented in 1622 by the English mathematician William Oughtred, and which is suitable for many rough-and-ready calculations but has now been almost entirely replaced by the pocket calculator. On the slide rule, numbers are represented by lengths; so much slide rule corresponds essentially to so much number. Generally speaking, analog calculators are limited in their accuracy by the precision with which measurements of length, volume, or other physical quantities can be made. In fact, most big modern computers are digital: they operate with digits in much the same way a human calculator does. Still using blocks but taking the digital approach, we would represent the number 1 by one block, 2 by two blocks, and so on, and addition would involve counting up the blocks. In a digital machine, there is no question of measuring anything; the only limit to the accuracy of the basic arithmetic processes lies in the number of digits that the individual machine can manipulate. To put it briefly: an analog calculator measures, while a digital computer counts.

One may wonder why an extremely high level of accuracy is needed. The first answer that comes to mind is that it is necessary in scientific and engineering applications. This is not really correct. A large modern computer does individual arithmetical operations that are accurate to many more decimal places than one ever needs in scientific work. This somewhat surprising point was emphasized by the late Professor John von Neumann in a set of published notes for a series of lectures—"The Computer and the Brain"—that he was preparing to deliver at Yale University just before his death, in 1957. Von Neumann wrote:

> Why are such extreme precisions (like the digital [computer's] one part in a million million) at all necessary? . . . In most problems of applied mathematics and engineering the data are no better than a part in a thousand or a part in ten thousand and often they do not reach the

level of a part in a hundred, and the answers are not required or meaningful with higher precisions. In chemistry, biology, or economics, or in other practical matters, the precision levels are usually even less exacting. It has nevertheless been the uniform experience in modern high-speed computing that even precision levels like a part in a hundred thousand are inadequate for a large part of important problems, and that digital machines with precision levels like one part in a million million are fully justified in practice. The reasons for this surprising phenomenon are interesting and significant. They are connected with the inherent structure of our present mathematical and numerical procedures.

Behind von Neumann's remarks is the fact that most numerical computations of the sort done on machines are necessarily approximate. The introduction of errors, even in a simple operation like multiplication, is inevitable, owing to the limited size of any given machine. As von Neumann put it:

Error, as a matter of normal operation and not solely as an accident attributable to some definite breakdown, creeps in, in the following manner. The absolutely correct product of two 10-digit numbers is a 20-digit number. If the machine is built to handle 10-digit numbers only it will have to disregard the last 10 digits of this 20-digit number and work with the first 10 digits alone. If, on the other hand, the machine can handle 20-digit numbers, then the multiplication of two

such will produce 40 digits, and these again have
to be cut down to 20, etc., etc.

The "rounding off" of numbers produces an error,
and the error increases when the numbers are used
in the next step of the computation, where again the
result must be rounded off. In a long computation—
and most computations done on a machine involve
millions of arithmetical operations—the errors keep
piling up, and that is why each part of the calculation must be done with the greatest possible accuracy. Von Neumann pointed out that to produce a
final answer on a computer to an accuracy of one
part in a thousand, it is necessary to perform the
many intermediate steps to accuracies of the order
of one part in a billion. That is the degree of accuracy
that a typical modern digital computer can produce.

The abacus, which goes back at least to 450 B.C.,
was the first of the digital computers. It consists of a
frame in which wires with beads strung on them are
set in a harplike arrangement. The beads represent
digits, and the wires represent "places"; the abacus,
too, is limited in accuracy by its physical size. A
skilled abacus operator can maneuver the beads on
the place wires at enormous speed. A now almost
legendary competition took place in 1946 between
one Private Wood, of the American Occupation
forces in Japan, and a Japanese clerk named Masturaki. The two men were given a number of arithmetic problems, with Mr. Masturaki using an abacus
and Private Wood a hand-operated electric desk calculator. Mr. Masturaki won every time. (In an account of this contest, Dr. Bowden suggests that Mr.

Masturaki may have had Klein-like abilities and may have been using the abacus simply as a prop.)

The first truly mechanical computer—an adding machine—seems to have been designed in 1642 by the French philosopher and mathematician Blaise Pascal. Pascal's device was very similar in principle to the now archaic kind of machine I used for my thesis. The numbers, from 0 to 9, were engraved on a series of wheels. The first wheel on the right "stored" the integers 0 to 9, the second wheel the tens, the third the hundreds, and so on. To store, for example, 109 involved putting a 1 on the third wheel, a 0 on the second, and a 9 on the first. To add, say, 8 and 3, one stored the 8 on the first wheel and then turned the wheel through three places. This involved "carrying"—an operation that was done by a series of gears arranged so that they turned the next wheel. In 1671, Leibniz drew up a plan for a machine that could multiply as well as add, and in 1694 a machine embodying his design was actually built, although it did not function very reliably.

At least part of the reason for the designing of these early computers was the need to calculate tables of the elementary functions, like sines, cosines, and logarithms, that arose again and again in scientific and engineering calculations. It is hard to realize now, when we can reproduce such tables by pressing a few buttons, that a few centuries ago one of them could represent the lifework of a man. Concerning the introduction of logarithms, which were invented by the Scottish mathematician John Napier around 1600 and were first tabulated in 1624 (to fourteen decimal places) by Henry Briggs, Dr. Bowden writes:

The introduction of logarithms by Napier and Briggs revolutionized ordinary computing; our civilization, dependent as it is on navigation, surveying, and astronomy, could probably not have developed as it did without them. Briggs devoted his life to computing the logarithms which Napier had invented. Both men realized the importance of their work; when they were introduced in Edinburgh, a friend related that they gazed at one another in speechless admiration for a quarter of an hour before the silence was broken.

One of the most grandiose of the early nonmechanical computing projects was initiated at the end of the eighteenth century by the French First Republic. It was an elaborate program for the computation of mathematical tables by human beings. In a book entitled *Automatic Digital Computers*, Professor M. V. Wilkes, of Cambridge University, describes this almost Swiftian effort as follows:

> This project was organized on what we should now call production lines, and the staff were divided into three grades. First, there were some five or six mathematicians who decided the best mathematical methods and formulae to be used. Secondly, there were eight or ten computers who were competent to handle these formulae and to compute numerical values from them; their role was to compute "pivotal values," that is, selected values of the function spaced at five or ten times the interval required in the final table. Thirdly, there were computers of lower

grade, nearly 100 in number, who understood only the elements of arithmetic, but who were able, by following rules laid down, to perform the final stage of the tabulation.

Professor Wilkes adds, "Seventeen folio volumes were computed for this project but were unfortunately never published. In 1820 the British government made a proposal that they should be published jointly but nothing came of it."

Anyone familiar with the use of modern computers will appreciate the similarities that must have existed between preparing instructions for the hundred arithmeticians and preparing a program for a machine. In fact, this similarity was not lost upon some of the mathematicians of the early nineteenth century, and certainly not upon the English mathematician Charles Babbage. Many remarkable men have contributed to the art of mechanical computation, but Babbage must surely be near the top of the list.

Babbage was born on December 26, 1792, at Totnes, in Devonshire. He was the son of a banker, and he eventually inherited a considerable fortune, which he used to finance scientific experiments. He taught himself mathematics as a boy, and when he went to Cambridge, in 1810, he found that he knew more algebra than his tutor. At Cambridge, he and some friends founded an organization called the Analytical Society, which was to "leave the world wiser than they found it." There are many accounts of Babbage's career, but one of the liveliest is Dr. Bowden's, which forms part of his essay on the history of computation. After describing Babbage's work on computers, Dr. Bowden writes:

Babbage was full of most ingenious ideas; for example he devised the method which during the last war became known as *Operational Research*, and applied it to an analysis of the pin-making industry. A similar analysis of the printing trade led to results which so offended his publishers that they refused to accept his books. He said, "Political economists have been reproached with too small a use of facts, and too large an employment of theory . . . let it not be feared that erroneous deductions may be made from recorded facts: the errors which arise from the absence of facts are far more numerous and durable than those which result from unsound reasoning respecting true data." This last sentence might be taken as the motto of operational research workers the world over. One of the most remarkable applications which he made of the method was to an analysis of the economics of the Post Office. He showed conclusively that the cost of collecting, "stamping," and delivering a letter was far greater than the cost of transporting it. He therefore suggested that operations of the Post Office should be simplified by the introduction of a flat rate of charges, which should be independent of the distance for which the letter had to be carried. It was as a result of these arguments of his that Sir Rowland Hill was encouraged to introduce the penny post a few years later. He studied the records of the Equitable

Life Insurance Company, and published in 1824 the first comprehensive treatise on actuarial theory, and the first reliable "life tables." They were used both in England and Germany for half a century as the basis of the new and rapidly growing life insurance business. . . . Babbage had a lifelong interest in inventing and in solving codes and ciphers of all kinds; he made skeleton keys for "unpickable" locks; he devised the method, which is now familiar to everyone, of identifying lighthouses by occulting their lights in a rhythmical manner, and had the mortification of seeing the scheme used for the first time during the Crimean War—by the Russians. . . .

[Babbage] set himself up in private practice as a consulting engineer and became very interested in the development of the railways. He was a friend of Sir Isambard Brunel, chief engineer of the Great Western Railway, and helped him by inventing the dynamometer car, with which he could automatically measure and record the tractive force of the locomotive and the irregularities of the track. He used to run his special train on Sundays, as there were fewer other trains to compete with, but nevertheless the signaling system was so bad that he often found himself heading for another train coming directly towards him on the same track. On more than one occasion he owed his life to the remarkable acuteness of his hearing, which enabled him to get on to a siding and avoid a head-on collision. He suggested the use of the "cow catcher," and he devised the first speedometer; he thought that there should be one in the cab of every locomotive. On one occasion he found himself on Hanwell viaduct on a flat car with no engine, and by holding up a piece of cloth which he had with him he was able to *sail* across the viaduct. He remarked that he thought that he was the first man ever to do this, and it is likely that here again he established a record which will stand for many years to come.

Merely a glance at a portrait of Babbage indicates that he was not a man to put up with nonsense. One of his portraits hangs in the Science Museum in South Kensington; it shows him to have had a high, round forehead, sharp and wide-set eyes, a long, narrow mouth, and a stern, though not entirely humorless, look. He took vigorous swipes at most of the established institutions of his day, once remarking of the Royal Society, for instance, that he had tried to "rescue it from contempt in our own country, and ridicule in others," and he also carried on a lifelong polemic against organ-grinders and street musicians. Sometimes, his writings were testy and acid, but not always. After Lord Tennyson wrote "The Vision of Sin," Dr. Bowden tells us, Babbage sent this note to the poet:

SIR,

In your otherwise beautiful poem there is a verse which reads

Every moment dies a man,
Every moment one is born.

It must be manifest that if this were true, the population of the world would be at a standstill. In truth the rate of birth is slightly in excess

of that of death. I would suggest that in the next
edition of your poem you have it read

> Every moment dies a man,
> Every moment 1$\frac{1}{16}$ is born.

Strictly speaking this is not correct, the actual
figure is so long that I cannot get it into a line,
but I believe the figure 1$\frac{1}{16}$ will be sufficiently
accurate for poetry.

I am, Sir, yours, etc.

Babbage seems to have been inspired to think
about computers by the image of the hundred French
arithmeticians executing, machinelike, the commands of a few mathematicians. He puts the year in
which he first began thinking about mechanical computers at 1812, and recalls in his autobiography,
Passages from the Life of a Philosopher, published
in 1864: "One evening I was sitting in the rooms of
the Analytical Society at Cambridge, my head lean-
ing forward on the Table in a kind of a dreamy
mood, with a Table of logarithms lying open before
me. Another member coming into the room, and
seeing me half asleep called out, 'Well, Babbage,
what are you dreaming about?' to which I replied,
'I am thinking that all these Tables (pointing to the
logarithms) might be calculated by machinery.'"

It was not until several years later that Babbage
actually designed the first of his machines, the Difference Engine, which was completed in 1822. It
was a relatively modest affair—basically an adding
machine that was specially designed for the computation of polynomials, such as x^2+x+41. Babbage's
model worked to an accuracy of six decimal places
and was actually used in the computation of tables.

In his autobiography, Babbage gives an exceedingly lucid account of the principles of the Difference Engine. Lest the reader's enthusiasm for this difficult subject flag, Babbage encourages him with a quote from E. De Joncourt, an eighteenth-century professor of philosophy, who had published a celebrated table containing twenty thousand so-called triangular numbers (numbers like 1, 3, and 6 that can be arrayed in triangles . ∴ .∵.). De Joncourt wrote, "That sweet joy may arise from such contemplations cannot be denied. Numbers and lines have many charms, unseen by vulgar eyes, and only discovered to the unwearied and respectful souls of Art. In features the serpentine line (who starts not at the name) produces beauty and love; and in numbers, high powers, and humble roots, give soft delight. Lo! the raptured arithmetician! Easily satisfied, he asks no Brussels lace nor a coach and six. To calculate, contents his liveliest desires, and obedient numbers are within his reach."

As a next step, Babbage proposed to make a larger Difference Engine, which would be capable of working to an accuracy of twenty decimal places—no mean trick, even by modern standards. The British government contributed about seventeen thousand pounds toward its construction, but it was never completed. The engineering techniques of Babbage's time were not as far advanced as Babbage's imagination, and no one could make the levers and cogwheels with the precision he needed.

In 1833, Babbage conceived a new device, the Analytical Engine, which occupied him for the rest of his life, and which he never succeeded in building, either. The new engine represented a profound

conceptual advance over the old one. The Difference
Engine was designed to perform just the limited set
of operations necessary in computing simple polynomials; the Analytical Engine was designed to
perform any arithmetic operation at all and to string
such operations together to solve, in principle, any
conceivable arithmetic problem. In fact, the Analytical Engine would have had the sort of flexibility
that modern machines have, though it would have
functioned at a snail's pace compared to any modern
machine. Babbage envisioned that it might be able
to perform about sixty additions a minute. All the
operations were to be mechanical, and thus would
involve the machinations of a vast collection of gears
and cranks, which presumably were to be run on
steam power.

The mechanical aspects of Babbage's engine, ingenious as they were, may seem archaic today, but
his general conception of a computer, as we shall
see, is not in the least archaic. His machine was to
have four basic parts. There would have been what
Babbage called the "store," in which the numerical
data involved in a calculation would be placed. It
would consist of columns of wheels, each bearing
ten engraved digits. Babbage wanted the store to
hold a thousand 50-digit numbers. In trying to construct his store, he turned out thousands of superb
mechanical drawings and a variety of new machine-
shop techniques. The second basic part of his computer was to be the "mill"—the part in which
arithmetical operations would be carried out, through
the rotation of gears and wheels. Third, there was to
be a device—essentially a collection of gears and

levers—that could transfer numbers back and forth between the mill and the store. And, finally, there was a mechanism for getting numerical data in and out.

The best description of Babbage's proposed computer was given not by Babbage himself (for all his sharpness of tongue, he was, especially in later life, almost incapable of delivering a coherent account of the Analytical Engine) but by Ada Augusta, countess of Lovelace, "the only daughter of the house and heart" of the poet Byron. Lady Lovelace, who was born in 1815, early showed a considerable aptitude for mathematics. (She died at the age of thirty-six and is buried next to her father in Newstead in Nottinghamshire. She had been separated from him when her mother, Annabella Millbanke, left Byron when Ada was a month old.) When she was a child, she was taken with a group of Lady Byron's friends to see Babbage's Difference Engine, and one of them, Mrs. Augustus De Morgan, noted in her reminiscences, "While the rest of the party gazed at this beautiful instrument with the same sort of expression and feeling that some savages are said to have shown on first seeing a looking glass or hearing a gun, Miss Byron, young as she was, understood its working and saw the great beauty of the invention." Much of what is known about the principles of the Analytical Engine is the result of Miss Byron's interest. In 1840, Babbage gave some lectures in Turin, and in his audience there was an Italian military engineer named L. F. Menabrea, who was on the staff of the Royal Academy at Turin; Menabrea was so impressed by the lectures that he summarized them in an article, in French, which was published in Geneva in 1842. Later, Lady Lovelace translated this article into English and annotated it. Her article, with its annotations, is the best account available of the technical aspects of Babbage's Analytical Engine. Lady Lovelace described in great detail the method that Babbage had devised for getting data in and out of the machine. His plan was to take over the method of punch cards that the French inventor Jacquard had worked out for weaving patterns in rugs. The pattern of punches was used to determine which threads would be woven into the rug pattern at each pass of the shuttle, and the whole process was based on whether certain rods in the Jacquard loom did or did not encounter punches in the cards. Patterns of great intricacy were made on the Jacquard loom, and one of Babbage's most prized possessions was a woven portrait of Jacquard himself, which had required the use of twenty-four thousand cards. Babbage proposed to make a very similar use of cards to run the Analytical Engine, the chief difference being that the patterns of holes were to correspond to mathematical symbols. As Lady Lovelace put it, "We may say most aptly that the Analytical Engine *weaves algebraic patterns* just as the Jacquard-loom weaves flowers and leaves."

Anyone familiar with modern programming can only wonder at the sophistication of Babbage's ideas on the subject. In the first place, he saw clearly that by means of his cards he could program his machine to do most of its operations automatically. Earlier computers had been largely manual, and the operator had had to intervene physically at every step of the way. Lady Lovelace wrote, "This engine surpasses its predecessors, both in the extent of the calculations which it can perform, in the facility, certainty and accuracy with which it can effect them, and in the absence of all necessity for the intervention of human intelligence *during the performance of its calculations.*" Babbage also anticipated a number of specific elements of modern programming. For example, he recognized the utility of having special mathematical data stored in an external memory and accessible to the machine on call. If a certain logarithm was needed, the machine was to ring a bell and display at a window a card that would show which logarithm was needed. If the operator supplied the wrong value, the machine was to ring a louder bell. Today, when some quantity like a logarithm is needed, an electronic computer can ordinarily evaluate it afresh much faster than it can read the value from a stored table. This possibility was foreseen by Babbage. "It is an interesting question, which time only can solve, to know whether such Tables on cards will ever be required by the Engine," he wrote. "Tables are used for saving the time of continually computing individual numbers. But the computations to be made by the Engine are so rapid that it seems most probable that it will make shorter work by computing directly from proper formulae than by having recourse to its own Tables." Moreover, Babbage seems to have had a clear understanding of one of the most extraordinary and valuable abilities of automatic computers—the ability to perform conditional operations, such as those called for by the IF statement of FORTRAN. This is the statement that asks the machine to choose among steps, depending on what a previous step came up with—for instance, a positive or negative number. Since the outcome cannot be known prior to the calculation, either the machine must have some mechanism for making the decision and taking the appropriate next step or the operator must intervene in the calculation, thus slowing things down. Babbage's way of having his machine make this sort of decision was exceedingly ingenious, and is very similar in principle to the way modern machines make their decisions. To understand it, let us look at what happens when a larger number is subtracted from a smaller one:

$$\begin{array}{r} 000\ 216 \\ -\ 000\ 317 \\ \hline 999\ 899 \end{array}$$

The string of three zeros to the left of the 216 and 317 indicates that the size of the numbers we are considering is limited to six digits, and the array of 9s to the left of the 8 is the result of successive "borrowing" of 1s. If we were not limited to six-digit numbers, the string of 9s would extend indefinitely to the left. Ordinarily, one would write the result of this subtraction as −101. The number 999 899 is known as the "9s complement" of −101. It is easy to see that adding 999 899 to a number and throwing away the 1 to be carried at the end is equivalent to subtracting 101 from that number. For example:

$$\begin{array}{r} 000\ 317 \\ -\ 000\ 101 \\ \hline 000\ 216 \end{array}$$

And:

$$
\begin{array}{r}
000\ 317 \\
+\ 999\ 899 \\
\hline
000\ 216
\end{array}
$$

Many computers make use of the principle of complementing to perform subtractions by reducing them to addition although, as I will explain, these machines use binary rather than decimal arithmetic.

Needless to say, any given machine can provide only a limited number of places, and Babbage made use of this fact in designing his Analytical Engine to make decisions. Suppose that it carried out a computation and got a negative answer. It would then produce a string of 9s to the left until it ran out of places. What Babbage did was to conceive of an extra place, which would be used not to register another 9 but to set in motion gears that could activate some other part of the computer, which would thereupon select an alternate set of punch cards. In other words, Babbage's machine could modify its course of action according to the outcome of previous calculations. Babbage described this process as "the Engine moving forward by eating its own tail," and he intended to use it in, among other things, programming the machine to perform cycles of operations. If one wanted to perform a certain set of operations, say, ten times, one would put the number 10 into a special register. Each time the operation was carried out, the machine would subtract a 1 from whatever number was left in that register. The next subtraction after the tenth would produce a negative number in the register, and a lever action set up by the string of 9s in the 9s complement of this number would be used to stop the cycle and get the machine started in a new phase of its calculation. This sequence of operations, which resembles that called for by the FORTRAN DO statements, is embodied in all modern computers.

Babbage spent nearly forty years trying to build the Analytical Engine. He could hardly think of anything else. In July, 1836, one of his friends, a mathematician named Mary Somerville, wrote to another friend, "Mr. Babbage is looking wretchedly and has been very unwell. I have done all I could to persuade him to leave town, but in vain. I do fear the machine will be the death of him, for certain I am that the human machine cannot stand that restless energy of mind." In 1842, the government stopped supporting his projects (Babbage described the responsible Chancellor of the Exchequer as "the Herostratus of Science," who, "if he escapes oblivion will be linked with the destroyer of the Ephesian temple"), and he and Lady Lovelace spent a considerable amount of time trying, without success, to invent a foolproof method of playing the horses in order to raise money for the Engine. Later on, Babbage invented a machine that could play ticktacktoe, and he thought for a time of building it and exhibiting it in carnivals. As he wrote in his autobiography:

> It occurred to me that if an automaton were made to play this game, it might be surrounded with such attractive circumstances that a very popular and profitable exhibition might be produced. I imagined that the machine might consist

of the figures of two children playing against each other, accompanied by a lamb and a cock. That the child who won the game might clap his hands whilst the cock was crowing, after which, that the child who was beaten might cry and wring his hands whilst the lamb began bleating.

Having fully satisfied myself of the power of making such an automaton, the next step was to ascertain whether there was any probability, if it were exhibited to the public, of its producing, in a moderate time, such a sum of money as would enable me to construct the Analytical Engine. A friend, to whom I had at an early period communicated the idea, entertained great hopes of its pecuniary success. When it became known that an automaton could beat not merely children but even papa and mamma at a child's game, it seemed not unreasonable to expect that every child who heard of it would ask mamma to see it. On the other hand, every mamma, and some few papas, who heard of it would doubtless take their children to so singular and interesting a sight. I resolved, on my return to London, to make inquiries as to the relative productiveness of the various exhibitions of recent years, and also to obtain some rough estimate of the probable time it would take to construct the automaton, as well as some approximation to the expense.

It occurred to me that if half a dozen were made, they might be exhibited in three different places at the same time. Each exhibitor might then have an automaton in reserve in case of accidental injury. On my return to town I made the inquiries I alluded to, and found that the English machine for making Latin verses, the German talking-machine, as well as several others, were entire failures in a pecuniary point of view. I also found that the most profitable exhibition which had occurred for many years was that of the little dwarf, General Tom Thumb.

On considering the whole question, I arrived at the conclusion, that to conduct the affair to a successful issue it would occupy so much of my own time to contrive and execute the machinery, and then to superintend the working out of the plan, that even if successful in point of pecuniary profit, it would be too late to avail myself of the money thus acquired to complete the Analytical Engine.

By the time of Babbage's death, in 1871, the machine had eaten up much of his personal fortune. Some of its parts were actually constructed (largely by his son, H. P. Babbage), only to become museum curiosities, and a great many detailed drawings of other parts were made. His work was an enigma to most of his contemporaries, and since it was never completed, one cannot guess how they would have reacted to a large-scale computer. Lady Lovelace had some apprehensions about this, and wrote a commentary, which is still widely quoted:

It is desirable to guard against the possibility of exaggerated ideas that might arise as to the powers of the Analytical Engine. In considering any new subject, there is frequently a tendency,

first to *overrate* what we find to be already interesting or remarkable; and, secondly, by a sort of
natural reaction, to *undervalue* the true state of
the case, when we do discover that our notions
have surpassed those that were really tenable.

The Analytical Engine has no pretensions
whatever to *originate* anything. It can do whatever we *know how to order it* to perform. It can
follow analysis; but it has no power of *anticipat-
ing* any analytical relations or truths. Its province
is to assist us in making *available* what we are
already acquainted with.

I will come back to the issues Lady Lovelace
raised, but, in any event, Babbage's work was for-
gotten until the 1940's, when another generation of
scientists and engineers, struggling anew with the
problem of designing large-scale digital computers,
came to realize that Babbage, with all his gears and
cranks, had been there before them.

3.

Any description of a modern digital computer can, broadly speaking, be divided into two parts. One has to do with the machine's "hardware"—its specific electronic components and circuits—and the other has to do with its logical design; that is, the organization of the available components, whatever they may be. In practice, of course, the two aspects are connected; it would not be of much use to design a machine whose circuitry was beyond the scope of existing technology. The circuitry of any modern computer is extremely complex, and to understand it in any depth requires a good deal of expertise in electronics and electrical engineering.

However, one can understand much about the logical organization of the machines without knowing how all of the parts work in detail. In fact, Babbage's Engine had no electrical parts and yet its logical organization has a lot in common with that of the modern machines. Modern electronic technology has produced computer parts more efficient than even Babbage imagined, but they are put together in units he would certainly have found familiar.

All computers consist of four basic units. In the first place, there must be some mechanism for getting data and instructions into the machine and for getting answers out—the link, that is, between the machine and the human programmer. Today, there are a variety of methods for establishing this link. For instance, to consider just input, data may be recorded on punch cards, much as Babbage envisioned, or on magnetic tape, or in a variety of other ways which can be fed into the computer and "read" by it electronically. In any case, the numbers and letters in the programmer's language are translated into coded patterns, and the coded patterns, in turn, are translated by the electronics of the machine into patterns of electrical pulses. These patterns must be stored somewhere in the machine until they are needed, and thus the second basic element in the machine is Babbage's "store"—or memory, as it is called today. In most modern machines, the memory that stores numbers consists of a great many electronic storage units (I will describe some of the modern versions later) that respond to the patterns of electrical pulses. In the third place, the machine must have some arrangement for manipulating stored numbers—the "mill," or, in the modern phrase, the arithmetic unit. For example, if two numbers are to be added, there must be a part of the machine in which the actual addition can take place. Today's arithmetic unit is a complex of special circuits designed to combine the patterns of electrical pulses corresponding to the individual numbers into new patterns of pulses, corresponding to the results of the arithmetical operation. Finally, there must be an element that controls the entire sequence of operations. This control unit—another complex of special circuits—not only arranges for numbers to be brought into and out of the memory but guides the whole sequence of arithmetic operations, and it does all this on the basis of a program drawn up by a human programmer. It is one of the triumphs of modern electronics that circuits that can do all these things have been designed and produced, and it is a tribute to Babbage that he envisioned how the same things could have been done by a collection of gears and wheels and levers.

The first large, modern calculators that were actually built were of the analog type—machines in which the arithmetic operations are carried out in terms of physical measurements.

The modern era of mechanical computation began about 1925, at the Massachusetts Institute of Technology, when Dr. Vannevar Bush and some associates made a large-scale analog calculator. It had electric motors, but otherwise was entirely mechanical. The quantities being computed were represented by the number of degrees through which certain gears had rotated, and this meant that the accuracy of the computations was limited by the precision with which the angles could be measured. In 1935, the M.I.T. group began designing a second model, which introduced, along with other improvements, an electrical method for measuring the angles. This model was completed in 1942, but the fact was kept secret until the end of the war, because the Bush machines were extensively used for the computation of artillery firing tables. (A rumor was deliberately circulated that it had been impossible to finish the new model.) Computing the tables involved solving "ordinary" differential equations—equations with just *one* variable—and the machines were reasonably fast, by human standards; solving a typical equation, which might have taken a human computer a week, took the machines about half an hour. However, as is true of all analog calculators, there were intrinsic limitations to their flexibility. Most problems in physics and engineering involve the solution of partial differential equations—equations with *many* variables—something entirely beyond the capacity of the Bush calculators.

In 1937, Howard Aiken, one of the first modern computer pioneers, began work at Harvard on his Ph.D. thesis in physics. The theoretical aspects of the thesis involved the solution of so-called nonlinear ordinary differential equations, which could be done only by means of numerical approximation, and the computations needed to reach these approximate solutions proved to be extremely long. Aiken began considering possible methods of doing the computations on machines and soon invented a machine that would evaluate simple polynomials. After a year or two, during which he invented variations on this machine that would solve more complex kinds of problems, it occurred to him that all these machines were, in their logical organization, essentially identical, and he started thinking about the construction of a single general-purpose machine, capable of dealing with any of the problems. He was able to get support for his project from the International Business Machines Corporation, and in 1939 work on the machine—the Automatic Sequence Controlled Calculator, Mark I, as it became known—was begun at I.B.M. in a collaboration between Aiken and four I.B.M. engineers named J. W. Bryce, C. D. Lake, B. M. Durfee, and F. E. Hamilton. The Mark I was completed in 1944, and was put into operation at Harvard. About three years after Professor Aiken began working on computers, he discovered Babbage. He was startled to find that he and Babbage had been preoccupied by the same problems. As Professor Aiken told me many years ago, "If Babbage had lived seventy-five years later, I would have been out of a job." In fact, the operating manual of the Mark I begins with a quotation from Babbage's book: "If, unwarned by my example, any man shall succeed in constructing an engine embodying in itself the whole of the executive department of mathematical analysis . . . I have no fear of leaving my reputation in his charge, for he alone will be able fully to appreciate the nature of my efforts and the value of their results." When Professor Aiken first came across these lines, he felt that Babbage was addressing him personally from the past.

The Mark I was designed to perform computations by following automatically—that is, without manual intervention on the part of the machine operator—a sequence of instructions that had been prepared for it by a programmer. The instructions were fed into it on a punched paper tape, and the numbers on which the instructions were to operate were stored in registers. One might wish to give the machine an instruction like this: "Take a number out of Register 32, put the number into Register 64, and then read the next line on the coding tape." This instruction would appear in the form of the sequence of numbers 32647, in which the 7 was the code for instructing the machine to read the next line, while 32 and 64 referred to the "addresses"—the particular registers—in which the numbers had been stored. Computations were broken down into small steps, and each step had to be expressed in terms of the primitive instructions that the machine could follow. As machine computations generally involve an enormous number of steps, the programmer had to go about writing down meticulously a very long sequence of such instructions—a tedious business.

The Mark I was electromechanical; the basic operations were performed by mechanical parts that were controlled electrically. Typical of these was the ordinary telephone relay—a device in which a metal bar attached to a spring can be raised by the pulling action of an electromagnet. When the magnet is turned off, the bar falls, completing a circuit. Such relays were used not only in the Mark I but also in some interesting smaller computing devices that were under development at about the same time at Bell Telephone Laboratories, under the direction of Dr. George R. Stibitz, who, like Aiken, had been trained as a physicist.

Before returning to the Mark I let me note that in a letter Dr. Stibitz wrote to me many years ago he pointed out that as early as 1939 he had built a small computer, which he called the "Complex Computer," that used binary arithmetic—the system to be discussed more fully later—in which all numbers are represented by strings of 1s and 0s. This seems to have been the first machine to have used binary arithmetic. It was exhibited in the fall of 1940 at a meeting of the American Mathematical Society at Dartmouth. The machine, on this occasion, was operated from New York City over the telegraph lines. Thus it was also a forerunner of the sort of remote-controlled data processing that is now common. In his letter Dr. Stibitz noted, "One of the interested people in the audience who pushed keys in Hanover, New Hampshire, and got back answers from New York was Norbert Weiner."

The Mark I used about three thousand of the relays. Like most mechanical devices, and unlike the basic electronic devices of today, they were relatively large and slow. Each relay was about an inch long, and could be opened or closed in about a hundredth of a second. It took some four and a half seconds for the Mark I to multiply two 23-digit numbers—the largest numbers it could handle. What with its relays and other mechanical parts, the Mark I's calculating was audible. As a student at Harvard, I used to drop in now and then and have a look at it. It was situated in a red brick structure just behind the physics building, and when it was working, one could go in and listen to the gentle clicking of the relays, which sounded like a roomful of ladies knitting.

It would not be completely unreasonable to say that by the time the Mark I machine went into operation, it was almost obsolete. (This is not meant as a reflection on the machine; it operated for more than fifteen years and turned out quantities of extremely useful mathematical tables.) However, about a year earlier, at the Moore School of Electrical Engineering of the University of Pennsylvania, Dr. J. Presper Eckert, an electrical engineer, and Dr. John Mauchly, a physicist, had begun work on the ENIAC —the Electronic Numerical Integrator and Calculator. This was the first electronic computer, for instead of relays and other semimechanical devices Eckert and Mauchly used vacuum tubes. The current in a tube is composed of flowing electrons, and changing the tube's state involves stopping or starting the flow. These electrons have a tiny mass as compared to the mass of the iron bar that has to be moved when a telephone relay is switched. In a vacuum tube, very strong electrical forces are brought to bear on the electrons, giving them very high accelerations in extremely short times, and the state of the tube could be changed in about a millionth of a second. By the time the first model of the ENIAC was ready for operation, early in 1946, it was by far the most complex electronic device in the world. According to one account, "In addition to its 18,000 vacuum tubes the ENIAC contained about 70,000 resistors, 10,000 capacitors and 6,000 switches. It was a hundred feet long, ten feet high and three deep. In operation it consumed 140 kilowatts of power."

A large factor in the decision to build the ENIAC was military pressure. In 1943, the Moore School and the Aberdeen Proving Ground, in Maryland, were conducting a joint project involving the computation of artillery firing tables for the Army. The Moore

School contingent, which used a Bush analog computer and employed a hundred women to do hand computations as a necessary adjunct to the machine operations, was under the command of a young first lieutenant in the Army Ordnance Corps named Herman H. Goldstine, who had been an assistant professor of mathematics at the University of Michigan before the war. When several years ago I went to see Dr. Goldstine, who was at the time director of mathematical research at the I.B.M. Thomas J. Watson Research Center, in Yorktown Heights (he is now at the Institute for Advanced Study in Princeton), he told me that the results produced by the hundred women and the machine were not very satisfactory—that, indeed, by the time Eckert and Mauchly began work on the ENIAC the situation had become "desperate." Back in the summer of 1942, Mauchly had written an informal report on the possibilities of making an electronic computer. In the course of things, the report got lost. Early in 1943, Mauchly and Eckert reconstructed it from a secretary's shorthand notes, and Eckert added an appendix containing some explicit suggestions as to how Mauchly's ideas might be embodied in electronic hardware. Dr. Goldstine, who was serving as liaison officer between the Moore School group and Army Ordnance, decided to try to get the backing of Army Ordnance for the project. On April 9, 1943, there was a meeting—attended by, among other people, Colonel Leslie E. Simon, then director of the Ballistic Research Laboratory at Aberdeen, and Professor Oswald Veblen, of the Institute for Advanced Study, at Princeton, who was one of this country's most distinguished mathematicians—at which the potentialities of the ENIAC were discussed. After hearing about the machine, Veblen stood up and said, "Simon, back that thing!" The Army backed it.

Strangely, there was nothing in the completed ENIAC that could not have been put together at least a decade before the war, if anyone had had the incentive to do it. Early in 1962, Harold Bergstein, who was then editor of a magazine called *Datamation*, interviewed Eckert and Mauchly. Part of the interview, as published, went this way:

> BERGSTEIN: Since the ENIAC was a direct result of your efforts and government money during World War Two, when would you speculate that the [electronic] digital computer might have been invented (a) if there had been no war, and (b) if there were no Eckert and Mauchly to invent it?
>
> ECKERT: I think you certainly would have had computers about the same time. There are a lot of things which cannot linger long without being born. Actually, calculus was invented simultaneously by two different individuals. It's been the history of invention over and over again that when things are kind of ready for invention, then somebody does it.
>
> What puzzles me most is that there wasn't anything in the ENIAC in the way of components that wasn't available 10 and possibly 15 years before. . . . The ENIAC could have been invented 10 or 15 years earlier and the real question is, why wasn't it done sooner?
>
> MAUCHLY: In part, the demand wasn't there. The demand, of course, is a curious thing. People

may need something without knowing that they need it.

In the summer of 1944, the late Professor John von Neumann, who was then a consultant to the group engaged on the atomic-bomb project at Los Alamos, started working in the field of electronic computing; his job at Los Alamos was to find techniques for performing the immensely involved numerical computations that were necessary in the design of nuclear weapons. By any standard, von Neumann was one of the most creative and versatile scientists of the twentieth century. He began his career as a chemical engineer, and though he turned to pure mathematics and theoretical physics, he retained a profound feeling for engineering practicalities. Indeed, his contributions to computing machines ranged from articulating the general logical theory of their design to working out the details of the construction of specific circuit elements. Von Neumann was born in Budapest, and after receiving his Doctor's degree, in 1926, he was a *Privatdozent* first in Berlin and then in Hamburg. He came to the United States in 1930 and spent three years at Princeton University. Then, in 1933, he became one of the first permanent members of the Institute for Advanced Study (Einstein was another of the original members as was Veblen), and he remained there until the summer of 1955, when he was appointed to the Atomic Energy Commission. A great deal of von Neumann's work in mathematics was inspired by problems that arose in the mathematical formulation of physics. He was able to take apparently unrelated concepts in theoretical physics and organize them into beautifully compact logical structures. Furthermore, he was one of the formulators of the "theory of games," the mathematical study of the strategy for winning very complex games. The book that von Neumann wrote with the economist Oskar Morgenstern, *Theory of Games and Economic Behavior*, is a fundamental contribution to the field of operational research. Von Neumann had a phenomenal capacity for doing mental computations of all kinds. His thought processes were extremely fast, and often he would see through to the end of someone's argument almost before the speaker had got out the first few sentences. Recently, one of von Neumann's colleagues said in affectionate explanation of von Neumann's power, "You see, Johnny wasn't human. But after living with humans for so long he learned how to do a remarkable imitation of one."

During the summer of 1944, Goldstine ran into von Neumann in a railroad station near the Aberdeen Proving Ground. Von Neumann was also serving as a consultant for Aberdeen, and he and Goldstine knew each other slightly. Goldstine told von Neumann that the Moore School group appeared to be well on its way to building an electronic computer that would be about a thousand times as fast as any of the existing electromechanical ones. Von Neumann immediately became much excited about the idea. As Goldstine has put it, "Once Johnny saw what we were up to, he jumped into electronic computers with both feet." Von Neumann's enthusiasm for the prospect of electronic computers can be fully appreciated only if one attempts to visualize the degree of complexity of the sort of calculations that were necessary in nuclear weapons design. In a fasci-

nating description of von Neumann's life and work
which appeared in the May 1958 issue of the *Bulletin of the American Mathematical Society,* Dr.
Stanislaw Ulam of Los Alamos, a close friend, and
a collaborator of von Neumann's on weapons-design
work, wrote, "After one discussion in which we outlined the course of such a calculation von Neumann
turned to me and said, 'Probably in its execution we
shall have to perform more elementary arithmetical
steps than the total in all the computations performed by the human race heretofore.' We noticed,
however, that the total number of multiplications
made by the school children of the world in course
of a few years sensibly exceeded that of our problem."

Von Neumann began an active collaboration with
the Moore School group. At this time there were a
good many exchanges of ideas among the members
of the group, and it is almost impossible to give a
completely coherent account of who invented what.
(The most detailed account I know of is in Goldstine's book *The Computer from Pascal to von Neumann*—see Bibliography.) In any event, certain aspects of the work culminated in a series of reports
written by von Neumann and Goldstine, with the
help in the first report of Arthur W. Burks, who is
now a professor at the University of Michigan. That
first report, entitled "Preliminary Discussion of the
Logical Design of an Electronic Computing Instrument," appeared on June 28, 1946. Curiously, although it has turned out to be one of the basic papers
in the electronic-computing field, it was for many
years available only in the form of a U.S. Army
Ordnance Department report.

Perhaps the most important idea discussed in this paper is that of "the stored program." To understand what this means, it is helpful to return to the ENIAC. In the ENIAC, as in any other computer, there was a memory for storing numbers. These numbers were manipulated by instructions that were themselves stored in electrical circuits in another part of the machine. Before starting on a given problem, one had to figure out each of the necessary instructions and hook up the appropriate circuits by hand—an operation that was something like plugging up connections on a telephone switchboard. In fact, plugging up a problem on the ENIAC sometimes took several people several days and involved making hundreds of wired connections. In a stored-program machine, certain common and basic operations are built into the circuitry. Each of these operations is given a number, and the machine is so arranged that an operation can be called for by its number. The programmer, at least if he is writing his program in machine language, can draw up his program in terms of these numbers, which will then be stored in the memory along with the rest of the numerical data. It must be made clear in the program which addresses in the memory contain instructions and which contain data. Machine operation is divided into two kinds of time cycles—"instruction" cycles and "execution" cycles. During an instruction cycle, the control unit interprets any number brought into it as an instruction, and the instruction is "decoded," which means that the built-in circuitry needed for carrying it out is activated. During the execution cycle, the machine executes the instruction.

Generally, the stored-program machine proceeds

automatically from one programmed instruction to the next. However, the sequence can be varied by what is called "conditional transfer" of control. In a conditional transfer, the machine is instructed to determine the sign of a number that it has computed and that has been put into the "accumulator"—a special register in the control unit. To give an example: If this number is positive, the machine simply takes the next instruction in the sequence; if it is negative, the machine will take an instruction out of sequence, from an address in the memory that is specified in the program. Thus, a conditional transfer enables the machine to change the flow of its computation as it goes along. This ability is a basic feature of all modern digital computers.

Stored-program computers have an almost unlimited flexibility. Von Neumann wrote:

> Since the orders that exercise the entire control are in the memory, a higher degree of flexibility is achieved than in any previous mode of control. Indeed, the machine, under control of its orders, can extract numbers (or orders) from the memory, process them (as numbers!), and return them to the memory (to the same or other locations); i.e., it can change the contents of the memory—indeed this is its normal *modus operandi*. Hence it can, in particular, change the orders (since these are in the memory!)—the very orders that control its actions. Thus all sorts of sophisticated order-systems become possible, which keep successively modifying themselves and hence also the computational processes that are likewise under their control. . . . Although

all of this may sound farfetched and complicated, such methods are widely used and very important in recent machine-computing—or, rather, computation-planning practice.

In 1945, some time before the ENIAC went into operation, the Moore School group began working on the design and construction of a stored-program computer, to be called the EDVAC, or Electronic Discrete Variable Automatic Computer. It was completed in 1950 at the Aberdeen Proving Ground— and was still in operation there as late as 1962—but not by the original group, which had split up after the war, von Neumann returning to Princeton along with Goldstine, while Eckert and Mauchly began designing machines commercially. (The first stored-program computer actually completed was the EDSAC—for Electronic Delay Storage Automatic Calculator—built at the mathematical laboratory of the University of Cambridge. It went into operation in May, 1949.) UNIVAC I—for Universal Automatic Computer—the first commercial stored-program computer, was built for Sperry-Rand by Eckert and Mauchly, and upon its completion, in 1951, was delivered to the Bureau of the Census. (In October, 1963, UNIVAC I was officially retired to the Smithsonian Institution after more than seventy-three thousand hours of operational use.) At Princeton, von Neumann supervised the construction of an experimental computer that embodied his ideas on machine organization. It went into operation in 1952. Paul Armer, of the Rand Corporation, in Santa Monica, wrote some time ago in *Datamation:* "The machine (variously known as the I.A.S., or

Princeton, or von Neumann machine) was constructed and copied (never exactly), and the copies were copied. One version of it, built at Rand, was affectionately called JOHNNIAC (over von Neumann's objections). Most of the copies are still in operation, although the [original] I.A.S. machine now has its place in history at the Smithsonian."

Another very important idea that was discussed in the von Neumann, Goldstine, Burks paper is the application of the binary number system to computers. In daily life, we are accustomed to doing arithmetic with the decimal system, which employs the ten digits from 0 to 9. In fact, most of us are so used to this system that we find it hard to appreciate that its use in arithmetic is quite arbitrary. In the reckoning of time, there are residues of other systems; the number of hours in the day is counted by twelves (the duodecimal system), and the number of seconds in the minute by sixties (the sexagesimal system). The predominance of the decimal system undoubtedly has to do with the fact that the best-known counting instrument of all—the fingers on one's hands—operates by tens. Much the simplest system, though, is the binary. In it, all numbers are built up from the digits 0 and 1. In the binary system, as in the decimal system, the first digit is 0 and the next is 1, but there the similarity stops. To represent 2 in the binary system we must take the next-largest number that can be made from 0 and 1, which is 10. The 3 is represented in binary by 11, and so on, with the result that the numbers between 0 and 9 are reexpressed like this:

Decimal	Binary
0	0
1	1
2	10
3	11
4	100
5	101
6	110
7	111
8	1000
9	1001

To construct the next number on the list, a 1 is added to the previous number using the rules $1 + 0 = 1$ and $1 + 1 = 10$ and "carrying" whenever necessary. This number system may seem strange at first, but one soon gets used to it, and it turns out to be far and away the most sensible number system to use in computers.

One reason for this is that the basic electronic components of a computer are "bi-stable"; that is, they have an intrinsically binary character. A switch can be open or closed; a pulse can be present or absent; a vacuum tube can be on or off; electrons can be present or absent at a given site. All these devices thus have just two stable modes of operation, which can be made to correspond to the 1 and 0 of the binary system. Therefore, if an electronic machine were to store its data in decimal, it would need ten vacuum tubes, or other bi-stable devices, to represent the ten possible values for any one decimal place. Indeed, the ENIAC did use the decimal system in storing numbers. Although some applications of binary arithmetic had been made in the earlier relay machines—as I have mentioned Dr. Stibitz built a binary adder as early as 1939—it was only with the advent of electronic machines that the use of binary storage and arithmetic became common practice. The bi-stable electronic devices can be used to store binary directly, and essentially all the machines that have followed the ENIAC have made use of binary numbers throughout. The use of binary greatly simplifies arithmetical processes in the machine. Binary addition, for example, is very simple to translate in terms of electric circuits: $1 + 0 = 1$ means that when a particular circuit, designed for adding, is fed one pulse, corresponding to a 1, along with no pulse, corresponding to a 0, it responds by producing one pulse, corresponding to a 1. Multiplication in binary is equally easy. To see this, we have only to multiply 2 and 3 in binary— which means that we multiply the binary numbers 10 and 11:

$$
\begin{array}{r}
11 \\
10 \\
\hline
00 \\
11 \\
\hline
110
\end{array}
$$

The number 110, as we have seen, is the binary equivalent of 6. It is evident from this example that multiplying the 11 by the 0 in the 10 produces just zeros, while multiplying it by the 1 in the 10 produces the number 11 again. This is characteristic of binary multiplication, and makes the designing of multiplying circuits much simpler than it would be if the multiplication were done in decimal, in which each place in the product may have any of the ten values between 0 and 9.

In the parlance of information theory, the fact that a bi-stable device is on or off is said to constitute a "bit" of information. Thus, it takes at most four bits of information to store a decimal digit in binary. (For example, to store the number 8, which is 1000 in binary, clearly requires four on-off registers, while the number 4, which is 100 in binary, requires three on-off units.)

A "word" of memory in a computer refers to the number of bits that are moved in and out of a given "address" in a machine's memory in a single cycle. The word "word" has no universal meaning for computers; it depends on the construction of a given machine. But "microprocessors"—the minicomputers that are now so popular—commonly process information in units of eight-bit words, although sixteen-bit-word microprocessors may soon become standard. Since eight-bit words are so common in computers they have been given a special name—a "byte." Pocket calculators often use four-bit words, which have become known as "nybles" (nibbles).

We may now ask the question, "How many different eight-bit words are possible?" To answer this, one might proceed by brute force and simply enumerate all possible eight-bit words. For example 00000000, 00000001, 00000010, and so on. If one had the patience to continue this enumeration, one would find that $2^8 = 256$ distinct words can be made. (A sixteen-bit register can display 65,536 different words.) A typical microprocessor has about 16,000 eight-bit memory registers. (This is designated by stating that the machine has a 16 K byte memory.) This means that such a machine has about $2^{128,000}$ different memory states. For comparison with this number, physicists estimate that there are "only" about 2^{260} particles in the universe. The big machines have an almost inconceivably larger number of possible internal states than the microprocessors. This means that in a practical sense only a tiny fraction of the possibilities of such a machine can be explored even in the lifetime of the universe.

The ENIAC, as remarkable as it was for its day, was by modern standards a behemoth—a veritable dinosaur. In a recent article in *Scientific American*, Robert N. Noyce, one of the pioneers in the field of microcomputers, made the following comparisons, "An individual integrated circuit on a chip [I will describe what these terms mean shortly] perhaps a quarter of an inch square now can embrace more electronic elements than the most complex piece of electronic equipment that could be built in 1950. Today's microcomputer, at a cost of perhaps $300, has more computing capacity than the first large electronic computer, ENIAC. It is twenty times faster, has a larger memory, consumes the power of a light bulb rather than that of a locomotive, occupies 1/30,000 the volume and costs 1/10,000 times as much. It is available by mail order or at your local hobby shop."

What is called *the* transistor was invented in 1948 by the physicists John Bardeen, Walter H. Brattain and William Shockley, who were then at the Bell Telephone Laboratories. They were awarded the Nobel Prize in physics in 1956. In fact there is more than one type of transistor and properly speaking they invented what is called the "bipolar" transistor.

What is it and how does it work? The material of choice for making transistors is silicon, a common crystalline substance. The trick for turning a silicon crystal into a transistor is to deliberately introduce an impurity into the crystal; something that is known as "doping" the crystal. Two basic types of impurities are introduced: the so-called "n-type" and "p-type." For reasons I will explain "n" stands for negative and "p" for positive. Suppose, for example, the silicon is doped with phosphorus. The electronic structure of phosphorus is such that it contains an "extra" electron that does not fit into the interatomic bonds between the phosphorus and the silicon atoms. If a small voltage is now applied across the doped crystal this electron—and any others that have been implanted at the doping sites—will move, making a current of negatively charged electrons—an ordinary electric current. This is what is called "n-type" doping. On the other hand, if an element such as boron is implanted in the silicon lattice there is produced an electron deficiency at the site. Such a deficiency is known as a "hole." Now if a voltage is applied, an electron from another atom will move to fill the hole and this, in turn, will leave another hole. Such a progression of holes cannot, in its effects, be distinguished from a current of positive charge—hence the name "p-type." To make electronic components from transistors one constructs sandwiches of n-type and p-type doped crystals. Let us consider two examples both of which fall under the general category of what are called "semiconductors."

The simplest example is to make adjacent regions of n-type and p-type materials; say a block of n-type adjoined to a block of p-type. Now if a voltage of a suitable sign is applied across the entire device it will make the holes and electrons flow across the junction between the two regions in opposite directions so that a net current is produced in the device. On the other hand if the polarity of the voltage is reversed *no* current will flow across the junction. In this case the arrangement functions in a circuit as what is known as a "diode," a now archaic term which arose from the name given to the corresponding element in a vacuum tube circuit. To go from a diode to what is usually called a "transistor" one adjoins a third doped region to the diode. Thus, for example, one may sandwich a p region between two n regions. This arrangement can be made to function like a "triode"—to use the old vacuum tube language—and it can amplify weak signals such as those received by a radio antenna. In the vacuum tubes electrons were made to flow by heating the tubes and "boiling" the electrons off the metal surfaces. The early radios had to be "warmed up" before one got any sound out of them. All of this consumed a huge amount of power, but there is nothing to warm up in a transistor. It runs cold at a fraction of the power. The first commercial transistor radio, the so-called Regency, appeared on the market in 1954. Ironically, it was not a commercial success.

Modern computers make use of what are known as "integrated circuits," the first of which was developed in the United States by the Fairchild Semiconductor Company in 1959. The idea is to use a single chip of silicon, which is then doped suitably to make the various circuit elements, which are, in turn, connected by conducting materials such as aluminum. These are photo printed onto the silicon chip; the transistors and wires that connect them are so small that they can only be distinguished by looking at them through a very high-powered microscope. By the very early 1960's logic circuits were being put together in this way. In 1961, the Digital Equipment Company in the United States designed the first microcomputer. By 1963, the first electronic pocket calculators with semiconductor components were being manufactured although it was not until the 1970's that mass production brought the costs down to around where they are now.

One of the uses of these chips has been in the design of computer memories. A chip that has an area of a few square millimeters can hold about sixteen-thousand bits of information and costs something like thirty dollars. Along with this reduction in size there has also been a rapid development in the speed at which information is processed in the machines—the so-called "cycle time." Cycle times of between thirty and fifty billionths of a second are common and times of a billionth of a second are in view. These times are so fast that the fundamental limitations imposed by the finite velocity of light—or any signal—are beginning to be significant. Light moves at 3×10^{10} centimeters a second which means that in a billionth of a second a signal will move only about thirty centimeters. This imposes a limitation on the size that such computer elements can have. If they are too big, signals cannot propagate fast enough through them to carry out the machine functions.

In addition to the internal memories that are built into the machines and which goven the basic operation of the programs, modern computers also have external memories of almost limitless capacity. Nowadays these are usually stored on thin circular disks that resemble phonograph records. There are two common types: the so-called "floppy" disk and the aluminum disk.

The floppy disk is made of a thin sheet of Mylar plastic on which there is a coating of a magnetic material such as iron oxide. Information is coded in the disks in the magnetic material just as it is done, in principle, on a tape recorder. Typically such a disk has a diameter of about eight inches and can hold some twenty-million bits of information. The floppy disks are read by a magnetic head that touches their surface so that they are subject to wearing. On the other hand, there are the aluminum disks, which can be as large as fourteen inches in diameter and can hold billions of bits. Such a disk can be made to spin at some three-thousand revolutions per minute and at these enormous speeds a layer of air is set up between the head and the disk which keeps it from wearing. The external memories, however, can be read out in times that are only on the order of thousandths of a second which means that the information that they contain must be fed into the machine at just the right time so as not to slow up its operation.

These disks will, very likely, be replaced soon by "magnetic bubble" memories in which information is stored in moving magnetic domains—bubbles—below the surface of a chip. About a million such bubbles can be stored on a single chip. A few cubic inches of these bubble memories can store as much information as a conventional disk.

By themselves these developments in computer technology, as remarkable as they are, would not account for the ubiquity of these machines in contemporary life. But going along with this technology there has been a steady—even spectacular—evolution in the ease and flexibility with which we communicate with these machines. I began this book with a description of a FORTRAN class I attended in 1962. At that time the idea that one might have a home computer on which one could practice programming would have seemed like something out of science fiction. Then, FORTRAN, which had been developed in 1954 and was the first programming language to have been created, was the one that most scientifically oriented people learned when they first encountered a computer, and they learned it in a class like the one I attended. This is not what happens today. Although FORTRAN and its successors and variants are still widely used, most people, especially the present generation of young people who learn computer programming in school or at home on their own computers, learn the simpler language BASIC—Beginner's All-purpose Symbolic Instruction Code. BASIC was developed by a Dartmouth group in 1965 with the idea of creating a language simple enough so that it could run on a small computer with a limited memory. (Some of the things that can be programmed in FORTRAN are hopelessly complicated—essentially impossible—to program in BASIC.) It is not my purpose here to try to characterize the ins and outs of the various programming languages. Some one hundred and fifty of them are currently in use in this country alone. (For a reader who wants to know more about them I would suggest reading an article entitled "Programming Languages" by Jerome A. Feldman in the December 1979 *Scientific American.*) What I want to do here is to give something of the history of these languages. I will focus particularly on FORTRAN and its immediate successors since these were, after all, the first programming languages and I had had the opportunity to discuss their creation with the people who invented them not long after they had done their remarkable work, at a time when the excitement and novelty of it were still fresh.

To see what was involved in creating computer language, it is instructive to return to the era before there were such languages. To be as concrete as possible I will discuss the von Neumann machine at Princeton which went into service in 1952. I am drawing on material in Herman Goldstine's book (see Bibliography) to which the reader can refer for more detail. This machine had a basic vocabulary of twenty-nine instructions each one of which had a ten-bit code number. For example the instruction "clear the accumulator"—the register which functioned as a sort of scratch pad for calculations—was coded as the binary digit 1111001010. A "machine language" instruction for this machine was a twenty-digit number. For example

$$00000010101111001010$$

meant "clear the accumulator and replace what had been stored in it by whatever number was located in the memory address 0000001010." A program for this machine consisted of strings of these twenty-digit numbers. It is clear that constructing such a program was the job of a trained mathematician and that if this situation had not drastically changed very few people would be in a position to use a computer. Thus began the attempt to create programming languages that more nearly resemble our own.

The task of designing a computer language like FORTRAN was a very complex one. In the first place, an analysis had to be made of processes and steps that occur frequently in the solution of mathematical problems—operations like conditional transfer. To direct the computer to perform such operations usually requires several machine-language instructions. FORTRAN and the other programming languages consist of set phrases—for instance, IF, indicating a conditional transfer—which the programmer must fit together so that they express a method of solving his problem. These phrases must be translated into machine language, and the inventors of FORTRAN had to design a master translating program, itself written in machine language, which would instruct the machine to do this translation. The beauty of, say, FORTRAN is that once it and the translating program have been set up, the user of the machine can for many purposes forget about the machine-language instructions altogether. He can write his program in terms of the IFS and DOS of FORTRAN, and let the translating program do the job of producing the machine language. The programming language phrases have been so chosen that writing a program in them is not immensely different from the way one might write out such a program in English.

By 1954, when an I.B.M. team began work in New York on what turned out to be FORTRAN, there had been at least two attempts to construct programming languages. J. Halcombe Laning and Neal Zierler, who were working with the Whirlwind (an early vacuum-tube stored-program computer built at M.I.T. and completed in 1951), had formulated a translating program that accepted mathematical or algebraic statements reasonably similar to those of FORTRAN and produced machine-language programs. These programs were quite inefficient compared to the sort that could be written by a human computer, and the system was not used very often. Also, H. Rutishauser, of the Eidgenössische Technische Hochschule, in Zurich, had produced a fairly complete language for scientific computing, but the computer he had available was too small to use for translating. In fact, most of the people involved with computers in the mid-nineteen-fifties did not consider such translating programs a very practical possibility. The reason was partly that the job had never been done, and partly that even if it were done, the programs that a machine could produce for itself would, it was felt, be slower and less efficient than the ones a skilled human programmer could produce for it. As one of the men active in computers at that time told me, "In those days, when we talked of the users of a computing machine, we had in mind the trained programmer, who did the programming for the *real* user—the man who wanted his problem solved. It seemed clear that the work of a trained programmer could beat a machine-constructed program, and it didn't occur to most people that with automatic translators the real user could learn to code his own problem and become his own programmer."

As things turned out, the language that the I.B.M. group developed was so skillfully constructed that the programs it produces are usually competitive in efficiency with those of a human programmer. In the group's first report on the completed FORTRAN, which appeared in 1957, it cited a case history, with an appropriate caution:

> A brief case history of one job done with a system seldom gives a good measure of its usefulness, particularly when the selection is made by the authors of the system. Nevertheless, here are the facts about a rather simple but sizable job. The programmer attended a one-day course on FORTRAN and spent some more time referring to the manual. He then programmed the job in four hours, using 47 FORTRAN statements. These were compiled [translated] by the 704 [an early I.B.M. machine] in six minutes, producing about 1000 instructions. He ran the program and found the output incorrect. He studied the output and was able to localize his error in a FORTRAN statement he had written. He rewrote the offending statement, recompiled, and found that the resulting program was correct. He estimated that it might have taken three days to code this job by hand, plus an unknown time to debug it, and that no appreciable increase in speed of execution would have been achieved thereby.

Roughly, it takes between four and twenty machine-language instructions to cover what is conveyed by each FORTRAN phrase. The translating program itself consists of more than twenty-five thousand lines of machine language, and took the original group almost two and a half years to design. The first FORTRAN translating system was designed specifically for the I.B.M. 704—one of the first computers to use a magnetic-core memory. These core memories have now largely been replaced by solid-state devices. As the machines got faster and more powerful, it was possible to enlarge and refine the language, and by 1962 FORTRAN had gone through four revisions. It was extremely important that each revised version should retain enough elements of the prior versions so that programs written in the older language could readily be accommodated to the new machines. Computer programs are costly to develop. Billions of dollars have been invested in developing them. (In general, computer programs are not patentable. I.B.M. could have registered the name FORTRAN, although not the compiling program itself. The company felt that it would be to everyone's advantage to have the language used as widely as possible, so no attempt was made to register the name.)

FORTRAN is still the most widely used computer language for scientific and engineering purposes. Not only are there foreign-language versions of the instruction manuals for using FORTRAN but there is even a French-language FORTRAN, which contains words like LIRE, FAIRE, and ALLER, which the French FORTRAN translating program enables the machines to translate into machine language. Mostly, however, computers are used not for scientific and engineering purposes but for data processing—routine but essential tasks like making out payrolls and keeping inventories straight. The people who use them in this way have seldom had scientific or mathematical training, and while FORTRAN can be used by people without specialized scientific training, it is a highly compact and somewhat abstract language. Therefore, as soon as the value of FORTRAN had been demonstrated, there was a large-scale effort, involving many computer manufacturers, to develop a language that would be more directly suited to business purposes. Fearing a consequent Tower of Babel, the Defense Department, a very important consumer of computer time, called a conference at the University of Pennsylvania in 1958 of both manufacturers and users to study the feasibility of developing a unified business-oriented language. Out of this conference and various study groups that succeeded it came COBOL for "Common Business-Oriented Language." One of the features of COBOL is the high incidence of terms like "WAREHOUSE" and "PART NUMBER." The machine can translate whole sentences like "SORT INVENTORY FILE ON ASCENDING KEY WAREHOUSE PART NUMBER." Most of the major computer manufacturers have models that translate COBOL.

My own modest brush with FORTRAN gave me a good deal of respect for the power and ingenuity of the language, and when I decided to learn more about the history of computing and computing machines, I asked the people at I.B.M. if I might talk with some members of the team that devised FORTRAN. In 1962, I went to Yorktown Heights to see two of them—John W. Backus and Irving Ziller. Both Backus and Ziller got into computing in the early nineteen-fifties, almost immediately after leaving college. In the summer of 1954, Backus, who was doing programming research for I.B.M., requested the company's support for work on what was to become FORTRAN. The support was granted, and he was able to put together a small group, which gradually grew into a thirteen-man team. Backus said that when he and his associates began, they didn't have the vaguest idea of how the project was going to work out in detail; although, from a good deal of experience in doing machine computations, they knew in a general way what the essential ingredients of such a language would have to be.

One of their biggest surprises was the way the machine went about translating FORTRAN sentences. Often there were machine instructions that did not seem to arise from any given FORTRAN expression, and in some contexts a FORTRAN expression produced no machine-language instructions at all. (Ziller told me that they would put something in and then go around saying, "Look what it did now!") When the system was fairly well advanced, they began racing their FORTRAN programs against machine-language programs produced for the same job by a human programmer. They would actually run the two programs on the machine, with a stopwatch in hand, to see if the machine-produced program was significantly slower. In the end, they found that for most standard problems the machine-produced FORTRAN program was about as efficient as a good handmade program. (It was obvious from the start, of course, that there would be an immense saving in time in the preparation of the program by machine.) I asked Backus how he and his colleagues had hit upon the specific phrases that are now part of FOR-TRAN. He told me that members of the group would suggest phrases, and then by trial and error they would see if they worked out on the computer. After FORTRAN was released to the public in 1957, a number of minor flaws and deficiencies came to light, and it was about a year before most of these could be ironed out. As soon as the program became fully operational, in the late nineteen-fifties, Backus said that most of the fun and challenge of developing it were lost for him, and for a while he turned his attention to other things. He is an I.B.M. Fellow— a position that gives him complete freedom to spend his time as he likes.

Perhaps the most interesting programming languages that have followed FORTRAN are the so-called "list processing languages" of which LISP, for "List Processor," invented in 1956 by John McCarthy, now of Stanford University, was the first to be fully developed. LISP is the language of choice for artificial intelligence applications, of which more shortly. In a computer program chunks of information can be linked to other chunks in what are known as "lists." These lists can themselves be thought of as quanta of information and can be linked with other lists to provide new ones of increasing complexity. A LISP program manipulates these lists as units. One feature of these programs is that one does not have to state in advance, as one does in FORTRAN, just how much computer memory will be needed to do a certain job, something that is known as "storage allocation." For many of the more complicated programs one does not know in advance how much memory will be required and the list-processing languages automatically create memory allocations as they go along. They can also be used to design new languages by treating a whole program as a list and then manipulating it to write a new list-processing language in an ever ascending hierarchy of complexity. These languages have a syntactical complexity close to that of the natural languages and will make programming still easier when the next generation of small computers becomes powerful enough to use them.

4.

After one has learned something about the extremely rapid development of computers since World War Two, one inevitably wonders whether there are any foreseeable limits to their future development. In this connection, it is interesting to make a few approximate comparisons between computer characteristics and some of the characteristics of the human brain. The basic cell of the human nervous system is known as a neuron. When neurons are suitably stimulated, they absorb or emit nerve impulses, which travel along fibers called axons. A neuron is about the size of a large organic molecule—that is, about a hundred-thousandth of a centimeter in diameter—while the axons sometimes extend for several feet. The disturbance generated by the neuron travels along the axon as an electrical pulse; concurrent with this electrical activity along the axon there also occur chemical changes. The nerve impulses travel along the axons at various speeds, but the highest is thought to be in the neighborhood of ten thousand centimeters a second. This should be compared with the speed of light, which is also the speed at which electrical signals travel in a computer—about thirty billion centimeters a second. The human brain, which weighs about a pound, has a volume of about a thousand cubic centimeters and contains at least ten billion neurons.

It is difficult to compare this number with some suitable number in a computer. A possible comparison might be with the number of bits per square centimeter that can be retained in a silicon chip memory which is now approaching two hundred thousand per square centimeter. But the problem with a comparison of this kind is that to this day no one knows where and how memory in the brain is stored. It is known that it must be stored in more than one location and that it is unlikely that each neuron in the brain contains a copy of all or part of the memory. Our memory—or memories—are certainly widely distributed in the brain in several copies but where these copies are is still a mystery. And one also must keep in mind that memory is only one of the functions of the brain. Indeed, the brain's ten billion neurons are organized to do a whole variety of mental tasks. To oversimplify, it appears as if they act individually as switching units or relays. When the neuron is stimulated, it "fires"—emits an electrochemical pulse, after which there is a period of about a hundredth of a second during which the neuron cannot be fired again. In this sense, the neuron acts like a digital unit.

The nervous system exhibits not only digital aspects (the transmission of electrical pulses), but also analogical aspects (muscular contractions produce changes in blood pressure). Von Neumann, in an essay entitled "The General and Logical Theory of Automata," gave the control of blood pressure by the nervous system as an example of how the two are interconnected:

> . . . the mechanism which keeps the blood pressure constant is of this mixed type. The nerve which senses and reports the blood pressure does it by a sequence of neural impulses, that is, in a digital manner. The muscular contraction which this impulse system induces may still be described as a superposition of many digital impulses. The influence of such a contraction on the blood stream is, however, hydrodynamical, and hence analogy. The reaction of the pressure thus produced back on the nerve which reports the pressure closes the circular feedback, and at this point the analogy procedure again goes over into a digital one. The comparisons between the living organisms and the computing machines are, therefore, certainly imperfect at this point. The living organisms are very complex—part digital and part analogy mechanisms. The computing machines, at least in their recent forms to which I am referring in this discussion, are purely digital.

Von Neumann points out that in reporting a quantity like the blood pressure the nervous system uses a kind of code in which the size of the quantity is made to correspond essentially to the frequency of the pulses transmitted. The information is read by counting pulses, and this insures a high degree of reliability in the system. "If you express a number of the order of a million by counting and miss a count the result is only irrelevantly changed," von Neumann says. "If you express it by [decimal or binary] expansion, a single error in a single digit may vitiate the entire result." In sum, the nervous system behaves in part like a digital computer and in part like an analog calculator and, hence, there is a good deal of imprecision in any comparison of the brain to a digital computer. The basic reaction time for a neuron is estimated to be about a thousandth of a second, as compared to a few billionths of a second for an electronic-computer component. Hence, compared to a computer, the brain has a much larger set of components packed into a much tinier volume, but functioning rather slowly. This undoubtedly means that the brain operates by making use of as many of its components as possible at any one time. A system with a few very fast components will operate most efficiently by using them in rapid succession, or serially, whereas a system like the brain, with many comparatively slow components, will make up for the slowness by processing information in parallel chains. As von Neumann put it:

> The natural componentry [the brain] favors automata with more but slower organs. Hence it is to be expected that an efficiently organized

large natural automaton (like the human nervous system) will tend to pick up as many logical (or informational) items as possible simultaneously, and process them simultaneously, while an efficiently organized large artificial automaton (like a large modern computing machine) will be more likely to do things successively—one thing at a time, or at any rate not so many things at a time; that is, large and efficient natural automata are likely to be highly *parallel*, while large and efficient artificial automata will tend to be less so, and rather to be *serial*.

One of the active areas in present-day computer research is what is known as "distributed processing" in which many small machines are hooked together in a network that processes information in parallel. Such a network of specialized processors is certainly more "brainlike" than the classical serial computer to which von Neumann referred.

It has become clear not only that the number of neurons in the brain is very much larger than the number of components in a computer but also that the basic principles of organization must be very different. A computer is constructed according to a precise predetermined plan—a wiring diagram—in which all the connections between the components are spelled out in detail. A completed computer exhibits very little "redundancy"; that is, if part of the memory, for example, is removed, the machine simply will not operate. On the other hand, there is a good deal of evidence to suggest that there is considerable redundancy in the operation of the brain. Some of the brain can be removed without noticeably impairing, say, memory, and it appears, moreover, that, if necessary, different parts of the brain can sometimes take over each other's functions.

Since the brain, when damaged, has a tendency to repair itself, its organization is clearly such that the defective parts become as inconspicuous as possible. On the other hand, the computer, which must be repaired when it breaks down, is designed so that defects show up as conspicuously as possible— so that they can be tracked down and corrected. Von Neumann noted:

> The basic principle of dealing with malfunctions in nature is to make their effect as unimportant as possible and to apply correctives, if they are necessary at all, at leisure. In our dealings with artificial automata, on the other hand, we require an immediate diagnosis. Therefore, we are trying to arrange the automata in such a manner that errors will become as conspicuous as possible, and intervention and correction follow immediately. In other words, natural organisms are constructed to make errors as inconspicuous, as harmless as possible. Artificial automata are designed to make errors as conspicuous, as disastrous, as possible. The rationale of this difference is not far to seek. Natural organisms are sufficiently well conceived to be able to operate even when malfunctions have set in. They can operate in spite of malfunctions, and their subsequent tendency is to remove these malfunctions. An artificial automaton could certainly be designed so as to be able to operate normally in spite of a limited number of malfunctions in

certain limited areas. Any malfunction, however, represents a considerable risk that some generally degenerating process has already set in within the machine. It is, therefore, necessary to intervene immediately, because a machine which has begun to malfunction has only rarely a tendency to restore itself, and will probably go from bad to worse.

Although the brain is certainly a vast network of interconnected neurons it has become increasingly clear that a good deal of this network is not, as was once thought, organized randomly. From conception to birth about 250,000 neurons a minute develop in our brains until the final number of some ten billion is reached. Many of these neurons do appear to have specialized functions with specific neurons programmed to develop in specific regions of the brain. How all of this information is processed is a mystery, and what these functional units are is also a mystery. A perfect example of this problem is our present understanding, or lack of it, of vision. When asked how we see something, most people give an answer that goes along the following lines: light passes through the optical lens in the front of the eye. This light then impinges on the retina which is the actual organ that is stimulated by light signals. The common notion of the retina is that it is something like a television screen on which the optical images appear. Here is where the trouble starts with the usual attempt to explain vision—for who is watching the television? Once one formulates this question it becomes clear that, somehow, the physical image on the retina must get transformed into symbolic information in the brain—into thought. We can experience this transformation for ourselves. All one has to do is to look at one of those "optical paradoxes" which looks at first sight like a blur of lines and colors and then suddenly turns into a picture of Abraham Lincoln. How does this happen?

No one knows, but now thanks to animal experiments done by people like David Hubel and Torsten Wessel at Harvard one can at least begin to follow the pathway along which this takes place. The neurons in the retina fire at a regular rate until they are stimulated by light. Once stimulated the firing rates of these neurons are changed. But these rates change only if there is a contrast between the illumination of neighboring areas of the retina. Uniform illumination of the retina does not change the rates. We are therefore very sensitive to optical patterns with sharp contrasts in illumination. This is the first level of optical pattern recognition. The retina is essentially a two-dimensional surface but signals from its neurons propagate to a three-dimensional volume in the midbrain which contains what are known as "lateral geniculate" neurons, organized in columns. From there the information propagates to the back of the brain to what is known as the "visual cortex." It is interesting that this latter neural network, which appears to be where the visual information becomes part of our mental consciousness, is as far away from our eyes as it is possible for a brain cell to be. Sight becomes transformed into thought literally in the back of our heads. But how does this happen? Are there individual neurons that are specialized to make these transformations or modular groups of neurons or what? No one knows.

One approach to problems like this has been in the field of what is known as "artificial intelligence," a term that seems to have been invented by John McCarthy, the creator of LISP. As the term implies, artificial intelligence is the attempt to manufacture entities that people agree are machines but which produce behavior that people agree is "intelligent." This is now a vast field with important centers of research at places like Stanford University, M.I.T. and the Carnegie-Mellon University in Pittsburgh. Broadly speaking the work has been divided into two parts—"robotics" and "programming." Robotics is the ancient art of making a machine perform some kind of humanoid behavior. In particular a great deal of effort has gone into constructing machines that see and hear. One of the first examples of the former is the so-called Perceptron, which was the creation in the 1950's and 1960's of the late Frank Rosenblatt and his collaborators at Cornell. This machine, which was made up of photocells with random wiring, was able to learn to recognize certain shapes like, say, the letter "A." It had fundamental limitations and has, in recent years, pretty much been abandoned. Marvin Minsky and his collaborators at M.I.T. have attached robot arms to computers and by coordinating the arms to visual inputs, have enabled the machines to catch balls and also to construct geometrical objects out of building blocks. The machine can "look" at a model and then with its arm construct a copy of it. While this field was somewhat neglected in favor of programming in the 1970's, it appears to be reviving because of the industrial possibilities that such machines offer.

Programming is the art of creating computer programs—in the context of artificial intelligence—that do nonnumerical operations. For example Minsky and his students have constructed programs that carry out symbolic algebraic computations of enormous complexity, that can solve high school algebra problems stated in English, and that can perform credibly in intelligence tests where reasoning by analogy is required. In the 1970's Terry Winograd, then a student at M.I.T. and now a professor at Stanford, created a program called SHRDLU which not only could construct geometrical objects that were displayed visually on a television screen but could carry out, within its limited context, intelligent "conversations" about what it was doing. It could respond to commands like "Find a block that is bigger than the one you are holding and put it into the box," and one could ask it, "Can a pyramid be supported by a box?" to which it would respond appropriately. Winograd's program, which was written in a modified LISP, was so complicated—it involved something like a quarter of a million lines of instructions—that even *he* had trouble keeping track of it. It is clear that Lady Lovelace's characterization, "It can do whatever we *know how to order it* to perform . . ." must be reinterpreted. To make a computer operate it must be programmed, but the programmer does not, and often *cannot*, know how the machine will then proceed. The machine makes its own decisions as it goes along and in this sense functions as an independent creative entity. Whether all of this very impressive work has led us closer to an understanding of how our own minds work is a question that is hotly debated. I will come back to some aspects of this in the next chapter.

The application of artificial intelligence that is most widely appreciated by the nonspecialist is the use of machines to play games. At the present time the world backgammon champion is a computer program called BKG 9.8 which was the creation of Hans Berliner of Carnegie-Mellon. It beat the then world champion Luigi Villa of Italy in July of 1979 in a match played in Monte Carlo, which it won seven games to one. Computer programs now play tournament level checkers and chess. Since there is a good deal of misunderstanding of how this is done I will close this chapter with a brief discussion of the chess programs.

The naive view of these chess-playing machines is that they simply proceed by brute force. It *is* true that chess is a determinate game in the sense that every position will eventually lead to a win, lose or draw after a finite number of moves. If a computer could consider all possible moves after a given one it could invariably come up with a winning strategy. But the number of possible moves is so enormous that this tactic is a practical impossibility. In 1949 Claude Shannon, the celebrated information theorist, made an analysis of these numbers along the following lines. In an average position during a chess game the player to move has a choice of about thirty legal moves. His opponent has then a choice of about thirty legal replies so that after one level of exchange the number of options that must be considered are 30×30 or 900. But if we keep this up then in a typical game, as Shannon argued, there are about 10^{120} possible alternatives to consider. If we had a machine that could process these moves at the rate of one billion per second then it would take about 10^{111} seconds for the computer to examine all of these future moves and their consequences. The universe is only some 10^{17} seconds old, so clearly this is not the way to proceed.

What must be done is to program the computer to consider only a small fraction of the possible continuations and to consider these only to a limited depth—say two or three moves. In practice what happens in these programs is that a depth like two or three moves is chosen, then according to criteria such as control of the center of the board, mobility of pieces and king safety, some subset of the legal moves is selected for further consideration. Then each of these moves must be examined by the machine to find out what the best response of the opponent is and so on. In this way a sort of logic tree of rather limited possibilities is set up a few moves deep. This is not how human chessmasters seem to operate. They pick out, by some sort of instinct, a very small number of possibilities, dismissing the rest, and then consider these few moves and their consequences to a depth that can be many moves—many more than the computer will consider. There is at the present time no chess machine that can beat the very best human chess players. Tournament players are rated on a numerical scale. On this scale, for example, Anatoly Karpov, the present world's champion, is rated at 2,705 while the best chess program designed by Ken Thompson and Joe Condon of the Bell Telephone Laboratories has a rating of about 2,200, which means that it is better than all but about five percent of the tournament players in the United States. The system—known as Belle—is being upgraded from examining 5,000 positions per second to examining 15,000 positions per second. Its memory contains some 150,000 standard opening variations. Given this level of machine sophistication it seems to me, at least, that within the next few years chess and other games will go the way of backgammon and machines will be their best players. Whether people will then think it foolish, or unworthy, to spend time playing an "intellectual" game at which a machine can beat them, or whether the machines will simply be put aside and allowed, say, to compete only among themselves remains to be seen. These issues are a special case of the general problem of whether machines can really be "intelligent," which I will take up next.

5.

Apart from the physical limitations of computers, many people have wondered whether there is some intrinsic difference between human thought and the activity of a computer. In short, can machines possess "intelligence"? This is, to some extent, a continuation of the long-standing argument in biology between the "vitalists" and the "mechanists." The mechanists claim that the human organism is merely a machine—a very complex one, to be sure—while the vitalists claim that there is an essential vital force possessed by the living human organism and that this cannot be duplicated mechanically. The same controversy arises when people ask, "Do

computing machines really think?" So little is understood about the processes of human thought that
when the question is formulated in this way, it can
hardly be answered. (It is, of course, beside the point
that when we think, we think in a language that is
the language in which we speak. The connection
between that language and the actual functioning
of the neurons must be at least as complex and remote
as the connection between, say, a FORTRAN instruction and the operation of the machine circuits in
carrying out the instruction.)

There is, however, another way of putting the
question—a way that was suggested by the late Alan
Mathison Turing, the brilliant English mathematician who was born in London in 1912—that is
answerable, in principle: "Are the responses to questions made by a given computing machine indis-
tinguishable from the responses to the same questions made by a given person?" In other words, is it
possible to distinguish between a given computer
and a given person simply by communicating with
them? Turing proposed a game—now known as the
Identification Game, or the Turing Game—that could
be played either with three people or with two
people and a computer, and that could be used to
settle the question of the distinguishability of people
from computers. Three people can play the Turing
Game as follows: Assume one of the players to be a
woman and another a man. (The sex of the third is
irrelevant.) The man and the woman remain in one
room and communicate with the third player only
by means of typewritten messages. They disguise
their identity in the messages by calling themselves,
say, X and Y. The third player can ask the two

others any questions he likes by sending in a type-written questionnaire, his object being to find out whether it is X or Y who is the woman. The woman attempts to reveal her identity by her answers, while the man attempts to disguise his by giving false answers. The questioner must use a rather sophisticated strategy to learn the truth—for example, if he simply asks, "Do you wear a dress?" both X and Y will say "Yes," and he will be no wiser than before. Now, Turing proposed to let the computer play the role of X or Y and let the third player discover "which of the two, X or Y, is human." If the third player can't decide this, the computer has passed its intelligence test.

Turing even proposed, somewhat facetiously, the lines along which the questioning might go:

> Q: Please write me a sonnet on the subject of the Forth Bridge.
>
> A: Count me out on this one. I never could write poetry.
>
> Q: Add 34957 to 70764.
>
> A: (Pause about 30 seconds and then give as answer) 105621.
>
> Q: Do you play chess?
>
> A: Yes.
>
> Q: I have K at my K1, and no other pieces. You have only K at K6 and R at R1. It is your move. What do you play?
>
> A: (After a pause of 15 seconds) R—R8 mate.

The reader will have noticed that the answer to the addition question is wrong. Turing reasoned that a machine that was clever enough to play his game successfully would also have to disguise its arithmetic abilities.

Turing continued:

> The question and answer method seems to be suitable for introducing almost any one of the fields of human endeavor that we wish to include. We do not wish to penalize the machine for its inability to shine in beauty competitions, nor to penalize a man for losing in a race against an aeroplane. The conditions of our game make these disabilities irrelevant.

As yet there are no computers that can successfully play Turing's game, although in its very limited domain Winograd's program comes close.

Turing's great seminal work was done in the 1930's before modern digital computers had been built. I do not know whether he was familiar with Babbage's Analytical Engine. In any event Turing created a mental abstract of a computer which, as I will explain, is so profound that it embodies the general principles of *any* computer that has been or ever can be constructed. The so-called "Turing machine" consists of an infinitely long tape that is divided into identical squares on which symbols can be written. The tape is made infinitely long so that it will not run out of room to do its work. Each of the squares is either blank or contains a mark, say the slash:/. In addition there is a movable arrow that points to a given square and is moved back and forth during a computation. There is also a mechanism that can erase or print slash marks. The "machine language" for this machine consists of just four possible instruc-

tions, which we may call L, R, •, and / and which
mean

(1) L move the arrow one step to the left
(2) R move one step to the right
(3) • erase the slash if there is one
(4) / print a slash if there is not one

The machine begins in some initial state specified
by some finite sequence of slashes and blanks on the
tape and with its arrow pointing at some square. A
typical instruction takes the form "move one step to
the right and if this square is blank then repeat this
instruction or if it is not blank then go to the next
instruction." To make this as concrete as possible,
here is a sample Turing machine program to carry
out the multiplication $2 \times 4 = 8$. (To follow the
sequence of steps described verbally below the
reader may refer to the figure in which the operations of the "machine" are schematically displayed.)

We begin by assuming that the Turing machine
in this case has an initial state in which all the
squares are blank except 10, 11, 12, and 13, as shown
in the first line of the figure. We now outline a
sequence of instructions that will cause the machine
to double the number of non-blank squares, bearing
in mind that at each step the machine must be
given two alternative courses of action depending
on whether or not the slash lands on a blank or non-
blank square. The first instruction is (1) R (that
is, move the pointer one square to the right): if
blank repeat Step 1 (that is, move another square
to the right), or if not blank erase / and go to Step
2; (2) L: if blank print / and go to Step 3, or if not

blank reprint / and repeat Step 2; (3) L: if blank print / and go to Step 4, or if not blank reprint / and repeat Step 3; (4) R: if blank leave blank and go to Step 1, or if not blank reprint / and repeat Step 4. Now this entire sequence is repeated four times, after which the answer appears as a series of eight slashes, in Squares 5 through 12. (Unfortunately, for the pointer and the machine's imaginary fuel supply, there is no way in this somewhat primitive Turing program to stop the pointer; after completion of the fourth series, it keeps encountering blank squares, leaving them blank and moving one space to the right—on to eternity!)

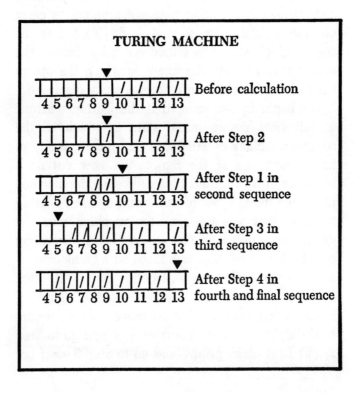

TURING MACHINE

Before calculation

After Step 2

After Step 1 in second sequence

After Step 3 in third sequence

After Step 4 in fourth and final sequence

Although all of this may seem primitive, Turing was able to prove some absolutely remarkable theorems about these machines. In the first place, he proved that in the mathematical sense there must exist universal "Turing machines." Universal Turing machines are Turing machines that can be programmed to do any computation or logical operation that any other Turing machine can do. In other words, universal Turing machines can be programmed to imitate any other Turing machine. In a book entitled *Computability and Unsolvability*, Dr. Martin Davis, of the Belfer Graduate School of Science of Yeshiva University, who is an authority on Turing machines, notes that "the existence of universal Turing machines confirms the belief of those working with digital computers that it is possible to construct a single 'all-purpose' digital computer on which can be programmed (subject of course to limitations of time and memory capacity) any problem that could be programmed for any conceivable deterministic digital computer."

In the second place, Turing was able to show that there were questions that Turing machines cannot answer. Of course, any *actual* computing machine

———

Opposite:

Stages of a program (a sequence of directions to the arrow to move one square right or left and to print a slash or erase one) for multiplying 4 × 2 on a theoretical computer invented in the 1930's by Alan Turing.

can be asked many questions that it cannot answer, simply because no one has devised a program for it that will answer them, or because a computation designed to answer them would be prohibitively long. But this is not Turing's point. His point is that there must exist problems for which programs cannot be devised in principle. An example is the so-called "Halting Problem." This is the problem of deciding whether a given Turing machine with a given tape will ever stop computing or whether it will continue indefinitely. Turing was able to show that there must exist at least one Turing machine for which this question is, in principle, undecidable. One cannot devise a program to determine whether or not the machine will stop computing. Turing's result is a variation on a remarkable theorem that was proved in 1931 by the late Professor Kurt Gödel. Gödel's Theorem showed that in a consistent logical system as rich as arithmetic there must be at least one proposition whose truth or falsity is undecidable. There simply exists no proof, and there cannot exist any proof, of the truth or falsity of the undecidable statement in the language of the system within which the statement was formulated. Gödel's result can be translated into the language of Turing machines, and if a Turing machine is asked the undecidable question, it will give either no answer or a false one.

Some people have taken Turing's result as a proof that machine intelligence, compared to human intelligence, is definitely limited. Turing himself did not think there was very much depth in this view, and in a marvelous essay entitled "Can a Machine Think?" he wrote:

Whenever one of these machines is asked the appropriate critical question and gives a definite answer, wc know that this answer must be wrong, and this gives us a certain feeling of superiority. Is this feeling illusory? It is no doubt quite genuine, but I do not think too much importance should be attached to it. We too often give wrong answers to questions ourselves to be justified in being very pleased at such evidence of fallibility on the part of the machines. Further, our superiority can only be felt on such an occasion in relation to the one machine over which we have scored our petty triumph. There would be no question of triumphing simultaneously over *all* machines. In short then, there might be men cleverer than any given machine, but, then again, there might be other machines cleverer again, and so on.

From 1936 through 1938 Turing studied at Princeton where he so impressed von Neumann that the latter offered him a position as his assistant at the Institute for Advanced Study. Turing declined, preferring to return to King's College in Cambridge. During the war he was instrumental in the successful project to crack the German military codes and after the war helped to design the first British computing machines. Von Neumann asked and, at least partly answered, a most remarkable question about Turing machines—namely, can a program be designed for such a machine that would instruct it to reproduce itself? It has always been assumed that machines could be used only to produce objects that are less complicated than the machines themselves. Only biological reproduction, it was thought, could reproduce complexity or even, by mutation, increase it. A machine tool, for example, by itself cannot make a machine tool. One must adjoin to it a set of instructions and these usually take the form of a human operator. Hence, the complete system is the machine tool plus the human operator. Clearly, this system will, under normal circumstances, produce a machine tool minus the human operator—hence vastly less complex.

Von Neumann discussed these matters in the Vanuxem lectures at Princeton in 1953, and since then these talks have acquired an almost legendary character. They were never fully recorded, however, though fragments appeared in a book entitled *The Computer and the Brain*, and they were discussed in 1955 in an article in *Scientific American* by John G. Kemeny, until recently president of Dartmouth.

When we discuss self-replicating machines we must be clear about the ground rules. In Kemeny's words:

> What do we mean by reproduction? If we mean the creation of an object like the original out of nothing, then no machine can reproduce, but neither can a human being. . . . The characteristic feature of the reproduction of life is that the living organism can create a new organism like itself out of inert matter surrounding it.
>
> If we agree that machines are not alive, and if we insist that the creation of life is an essential feature of reproduction, then we have begged the question. A machine cannot reproduce. So we must reformulate the problem in a way that won't make machine reproduction logically impossible.

We must omit the word "living." We shall ask that the machine create a new organism like itself out of simple parts contained in the environment.

Von Neumann showed, as early as 1948, that any self-replicating apparatus must necessarily contain the following elements: 1) There must be the raw materials. In his abstract example, these are just squares of paper—"cells"—waiting around to be organized. 2) Then we need the program that supplies instructions. 3) There must be a "factory"—an automaton that follows the instructions and takes the waiting cells and puts them together according to a program. Since we want to end up with a machine that, like the original, contains a blueprint of itself, we must have a duplicator, a sort of Xerox machine that takes any instruction and makes a copy. 4) Finally, we must have a supervisor. Each time the supervisor receives an instruction, it has it copied and then gives it to the factory to be acted on. Hence, once the thing gets going it will duplicate itself, and, indeed, von Neumann produced an abstract model containing some 200,000 cells which theoretically did just this.

Those who have had some education in modern genetic theory may have heard bells going off, or had the sense of *déjà vu*, upon reading the above description. It could apply as well, in abstract outline, to biological reproduction. We are, by now, so used to the idea of computer analogies to biological systems that they may appear obvious. One must keep in mind that they were not obvious at all; indeed, they are only a few decades old. Von Neumann's analysis was five years ahead of the discovery of the double-helix structure of DNA, and preceded by several more years the full unfolding of what is called the "central dogma" of genetic replication. In a Vanuxem lecture in 1970, Freeman Dyson of the Institute for Advanced Study made a sort of glossary translation from von Neumann's machine to its biological counterpart. The "factory" is the ribosomes; the copying machine is the enzymes RNA and DNA polymerase; the supervisor is the repressor and depressor control molecules; and the plan itself is the RNA and DNA. Von Neumann was there first.

His early training in Budapest was as a chemical engineer, and he never lost his feeling for engineering practicalities. He was not content to think purely in the abstract. Hence, he raised the following question: Real automatons, including biological ones, are subject to error. There is a risk of failure in each of the basic operations—a wire can come loose. How can one design a system that will be reliable even if the basic operations are not completely reliable? The secret was *redundancy*. Suppose, to take an example from Goldstine, one has three identical machines, each of which makes a long calculation in which each machine makes, on the average, one hundred errors. The way to improve reliability is to connect the machines, and require them to agree on one step before they go on to the next. If the system were set up so that once two machines agreed they could set the third at the agreed value and then proceed, then it turns out that the chance of error would be reduced from 1 in 100 to 1 in 33 million! Von Neumann concluded that the central nervous system must be organized redundantly to make it function at a suitable error level. This conclusion also appears to be correct. Von Neumann realized, too, that if the universal Turing machine could be made to reproduce itself, it could evolve. If the program was changed, say, by "mutation," and this change was such that the machine could still reproduce, it would produce an altered offspring.

In Freeman Dyson's words, "Von Neumann believed that the possibility of a universal automaton was ultimately responsible for the possibility of indefinitely continued biological evolution. In evolving from simpler to more complex organisms, you do not have to redesign the basic biochemical machinery as you go along. You have only to modify and extend the genetic instructions. . . . Everything we have learned about evolution since 1948 tends to confirm that von Neumann was right."

Von Neumann's complex arguments have now been greatly simplified by his successors. Abstract models of self-reproducing machines have been devised that are extremely simple. Moreover, real computing machines have elements in their design that are beginning to resemble self-replication. One uses a computer to program the design of a computer, and this design is given to a computer that supervises the actual physical construction of the new computer. One must supply from the outside the actual silicon chips on which the circuitry is printed, so, in this sense, the process is not really self-contained. Most people now agree that a truly self-replicating automaton would have to be the size of a factory (one of whose functions would be the manufacture of silicon chips). It now seems conceivable—in principle, at least, the logic is there—that the process can be further developed to the stage where self-producing automatons can be made that are compact and, acting in concert, can do just about anything. In his Vanuxem lecture, Dyson gives several examples of what colonies of these machines might accomplish, for good or evil, if let loose on earth or in outer space—such as bringing vegetation, light, and heat to Mars. With a little thought the reader can supply his own examples. For some reason, as admiring as I am of the logic of automatons, I find the prospect chilling.

I suspect—and this is also emphasized in Dyson's lecture—that for self-reproducing machines to do anything interesting they must have a very high level of interorganization. As Dyson put it: "The fully developed colony must be as well-coordinated as the cells of a bird. There must be automata with specialized functions corresponding to muscle, liver, and nerve cell. There must be high-quality sense organs and a central battery of computers performing the functions of a brain," which may mutate and proliferate. In time, we may no longer recognize them and, indeed, computing machines may begin to surpass our understanding of them.

In this respect, Sara Turing, in a lovely book she wrote about her son's life—Turing died tragically, perhaps by suicide, in 1954; he was forty-two—quotes a letter that she received from the wife of one of Turing's closest colleagues, M. H. A. Newman. Mrs. Newman wrote: "I remember sitting in our garden at Bowdon about 1949 while Alan and my husband discussed the machine and its future activities. I couldn't take part in the discussion and it was one of many that had passed over my head, but

suddenly my ear picked up a remark which sent a
shiver down my back. Alan said reflectively, 'I suppose, when it gets to that stage, we shan't know how
it does it.' "

A Selected Bibliography

(I have selected for this bibliography only those books and articles that I felt would be readable for someone without an extensive technical background.)

I

The FORTRAN Language

Clear accounts of the details of the language are given in: *A* FORTRAN *Primer,* Elliot I. Organick. Reading, Mass.: Addison-Wesley, 1963; I.B.M. FORTRAN manual—F28-8074-1 (1961). Programming Systems Publications, I.B.M. Corporation, P.O. Box 390, Poughkeepsie, N.Y.

Innumerable books are now available about BASIC, COBOL and many of the other programming languages.

II

Babbage, and Lady Lovelace
Faster Than Thought—Edited by B. V. Bowden. London: Sir Isaac Pitman & Sons, 1953. The essays in Dr. Bowden's collection give a good account of the field of automatic computation as it was in 1953. His own essays on Babbage and the history of computation are both informative and delightful.

Charles Babbage and His Calculating Engines. Selected writing by Charles Babbage and Others. Edited and with an introduction by Philip and Emily Morrison. New York: Dover Publications, Inc., 1961. The Morrisons' collection of Babbagenia is a splendid source of material by and about the great man. Large portions of *Passages from the Life of a Philosopher* are reproduced, and the Morrisons have written a fascinating historical introduction to his work.

Irascible Genius, Maboth Moseley. Chicago: Regnery, 1970. This is a valuable full-scale biography of Babbage with much about Lady Lovelace and the Analytical Engine.

III

Computing Machines
Essentially, all texts on modern computers require a considerable background in electronics to make much out of them. The ones listed were among the most readable for me.

Automatic Digital Computers, M. V. Wilkes. New

York: Wiley, 1956. Although much of this book is quite technical, Mr. Wilkes also deals with the history of the machines and the comparison between the modern computers and the Analytical Engine.

Giant Brains, Edmund C. Berkeley. New York: Science Editions, 1961. Mr. Berkeley's book is mostly concerned with the generation of computers that were built before 1950. His book gives a detailed account of the early relay computers as well as the Bush analog calculator.

The Computer from Pascal to von Neumann, Herman Goldstine. Princeton: Princeton University Press, 1972. Dr. Goldstine, who was present at its creation, has given a full discussion of ENIAC and its immediate successors, and predecessors.

"Preliminary Discussion of the Logical Design of an Electronic Computing Instrument," by A. W. Burks, H. H. Goldstine and J. von Neumann. This classic paper in the field of electronic computing was reprinted in an abbreviated form in the September and October 1962 issues of *Datamation* magazine. The reprint, annotated by Paul Armer of the Rand Corporation, is especially useful since Mr. Armer has retained those parts of the original paper that contain ideas still widely used. Much of the discussion can be followed by an interested lay reader.

Microelectronics. San Francisco: W. H. Freeman and Co., 1977. This is a collection of articles taken from the *Scientific American* that covers the new solid-state computer technology. So much is happening in this field that one must follow new developments by reading the daily newspapers.

Mathematics and Computers, George R. Stibitz and Jules A. Larrivee. New York: McGraw-Hill,

1957. This book deals, in a semipopular way, with a number of aspects of computers and numerical analysis. The emphasis is on the logical and mathematical facets of the subject. Mr. Stibitz was one of the pioneers in the field of relay computers and some of the book describes his early work.

John von Neumann (1903-1957)

There is as yet no real biography of this extraordinary man. Shortly after his death, the *Bulletin of the American Mathematical Society* devoted an entire issue (Vol. 64, No. 3, Part 2, May 1958) to his life and career. In the issue, there is a long biographical sketch written by Dr. Stanislaw Ulam, who was for many years a close friend and colleague of von Neumann's. There is also an excellent summary by Dr. Claude Shannon of von Neumann's contribution to the theory of Automata.

IV

The Computer and the Brain

A vast amount has been written on this fascinating subject. The following references were most useful to me.

The Computer and the Brain, John von Neumann. New Haven, Conn.: Yale University Press, 1958. Part of this book is in finished form and part consists of fragments that were written at the end of von Neumann's life. All of the book repays careful reading.

Information Storage and Neural Control. Compiled and edited by William S. Fields and Walter Abbot. Springfield, Ill.: Charles C. Thomas, 1963. This book presents a collection of essays on information processing in nervous systems. The level is technical.

"The General and Logical Theory of Automata," by John von Neumann. This fascinating and profound essay is reprinted in Volume 4 of *The World of Mathematics*, edited by James Newman. New York: Simon and Schuster, 1956. Von Neumann's essay covers all of the aspects of the relation between the computer and the brain that are treated in this book.

Gödel, Escher, Bach, Douglas R. Hofstadter. New York: Basic Books, 1979. This book is a true *tour de force* of popular scientific explanation. In it the reader can learn about Turing machines, the brain, artificial intelligence and God knows what else. There is also a monumental bibliography for the reader who wants to know more.

Machines Who Think, Pamela McCorduck. San Francisco: W. H. Freeman, 1979. This book describes the development of artificial intelligence and some of the reactions to it. It also gives some very sharp portraits of the human players in this game.

Index